D0929944

# BIRKENAU

## The Camp of Death

Judaic Studies Series

Leon J. Weinberger, General Editor

# BIRKENAU

## The Camp of Death

Marco Nahon, M.D.

Translated from the French by
Jacqueline Havaux Bowers

Edited and with an Introduction by
Steven Bowman

The University of Alabama Press
Tuscaloosa and London

∞

The paper on which this book is printed meets the minimum requirements
of American National Standard for Information Science-Permanence of Paper for Printed Library Materials, ANSI A39.48-1984.

Library of Congress Cataloging-in-Publication Data
Nahon, Marco, 1895-
Birkenau, the camp of death / Marco Nahon : translated from the
French by Jacqueline Havaux Bowers :
edited and with an introduction by Steven
Bowman.
p.      cm. — (Judaic studies series)
Bibliography: p.
Includes index.
ISBN 0-8173-0449-5 (alk. paper)
1. Brzezinka (Poland : Concentration camp)   2. Auschwitz (Poland :
Concentration camp)   3. Holocaust, Jewish (1939-1945)—Greece—
Personal narratives.   4. Jews—Greece—Persecutions.   5. Nahon,
Marco, 1895-    .   6. Greece—Ethnic relations.   I. Title.
II. Series.
D805.P7N34     1989
940.54-72-43094386—dc19
89-4661
CIP

British Library Cataloguing-in-Publication Data available

On the serenity of the soul of
my wife and little daughter,
my mother and father, my four sisters and brother,
and my nephews, nieces, uncles, aunts, and cousins,
and on the final peace of the souls of more than
forty of my immediate relatives murdered by the
Germans at Birkenau-Auschwitz,
I do solemnly swear that the facts
related here are the tragic truth.

*Marco Nahon, M.D.*

Deportation Route of
the Final Transport

Baltic
Sea

U.S.S.R.

Danzig
Stutthof

Vistula R.

POLAND

Warsaw

Berlin

GERMANY

Lublin

Erfurt
Gotha
Ordruf

Weimar
Buchenwald

Krakow
Birkenau-Auschwitz

Flossenberg

CZECHOSLOVAKIA

Echterdingen
Stuttgart
Dachau
Munich

Vienna

SWITZ.

AUSTRIA

HUNGARY

ROMANIA

Black
Sea

ITALY

YUGOSLAVIA

BULGARIA

Sofia

Istanbul

Demotika

Mouries

ALBANIA

Salonika

TURKEY

Mytilini

GREECE

Corfu

Athens

# Contents

# Preface

Dr. Nahon is a Jew of Greek nationality who once practiced medicine in his native country with an M.D. degree from the Faculté Française de Médecine et de Pharmacie at the University of Beirut, Lebanon. He suffered the fate of most of the Jews in the countries occupied by Hitler during World War II: with all of his family he was deported to the annihilation camp of Auschwitz-Birkenau, which he and his son alone survived. They now live in the United States.

Dr. Nahon has told the story of his experience with objectivity as a prime concern. During his captivity he believed that he would be obligated to do so if he ever emerged alive. Dr. Nahon strongly feels, as we do, that this true account deserves to take its place in the gruesome record of war lest we forget.

A typescript copy of the French original was deposited by the author in the archives of Yad Vashem in Jerusalem, where Steven Bowman read it in 1978 during the course of his initial researches into the tragic fate of Greek Jews during World War II. Several years later, Bowman learned from Nora Levin of Gratz College that Dr. Nahon was still alive at ninety-two and was living in Philadelphia, Pennsylvania. An interview with Dr. Nahon was arranged, at which time a first-draft translation of the memoir was obtained with the intent to submit it to the University of Alabama Press for publication in its Judaica series. The original translator was asked to prepare the revised version, which is now the text of the present volume.

During the course of several interviews with Dr. Nahon, numerous biographical details were revealed which illuminate his prewar career and the early history of this memoir. Some of his biography is included in the translator's introduction and in the editor's postscript following the memoir. Here the factors that led him to Beirut may be briefly summarized.

Dhidhimoteichon (Dimotika) was occupied by Bulgaria in 1915 in return for its alliance with Turkey during World War I. During their withdrawal across the Evros River, the Turks took all of the city's documents. The Bulgarians in turn registered all the males over seventeen. A number of Dhidhimoteichon Jews were subsequently drafted into the Bulgarian army. The Jewish community requested their coreligionists in Sofia to send them a teacher of Hebrew and Bulgarian. Young Marco escaped to Xanthi, and his brother Nissim registered in his place. He worked in a tobacco company for two years and was then drafted for the army, since his age was listed as nineteen (he was actually twenty-one). After induction he was stationed near Philippopolis. During a leave in Dhidhimoteichon, he found the opportunity to escape to Istanbul, and from there he went to Beirut to study medicine. He was to pratice medicine in his native town until spring 1943.

The original French manuscript was serialized in the Greek translation of Asher Moisis immediately after the war. In both languages the memoir deserves mention as one of the first Holocaust memoirs to be written and published. As the years passed, the importance of this document became more and more evident. It became obvious that such tragic memories should be preserved in print for readers of English as well as for readers of Greek and French.

We thank Edward Ginsburg for his help in preparing parts of this translation and Marcia Brubeck for her editorial assistance. In deference to American readers of

English, customary units of measure replace metric units in the original text. Dr. Nahon's transliterations of Greek place names have been retained in the text even where these differ from the spellings used in the introductions and on the maps.

Jacqueline Havaux Bowers
Steven B. Bowman

# Translator's Introduction

In the little town of Tubize, not far from Brussels, Belgium, my family, neighbors, and friends were counting their blessings. We had just survived World War II and the Nazi occupation. The Germans were finally gone. Gone too were the air raids, the buzz bombs, the shelters, the Gestapo, the reprisals, the curfews, the fears, the food rationing, and the privations. We had been liberated by the British and American troops amid the greatest rejoicing that I have ever witnessed. We owed everything, indeed our lives, to the brave soldiers who had come to liberate us from the Nazi yoke.

It was 1945. The people of our town, although still stunned, began openly discussing the terrible events of the past five years. We knew very little about the fate of the Jews. There had been few Jews in our town, but many had lived in nearby Brussels. I knew, for instance, that, through his office at the papermill, my father had been indirectly helping a Jew in hiding. This Jew had a fair complexion and blond hair. Everyone at the office, including my father, had been afraid of this man at first because he was an outsider with a German name and background. He had been trusting enough to tell my father that he ardently wished for Hitler's downfall, that he was a Jew. In addition, some of the children on our street knew that a little Jewish girl was being hidden by non-Jewish neighbors on the next street and that the Germans had come to look for her. We children had even practiced how we would lie to the Germans if they asked us her whereabouts. Our parents had urged us to do so.

Increasingly unbelievable reports of recent German

atrocities, many of them perpetrated against the Jews, reached our ears every day. I saw the brother-in-law of Léon, a close friend and fellow member of our little Protestant church, being brought back home one day. I rushed to tell my parents. I will never forget the way he looked: like a skeleton covered with skin. He was returning from a "concentration camp." I had never before heard of such a camp. René started telling all of us about the fate of two other non-Jewish young friends of our family, André and Joseph, who had been exterminated at Buchenwald. Some of the grownups did not want us children to listen. Henri, a man who lived on one of the main streets and owned a radio shop, became so upset and angry by the reports of eyewitnesses that he placed enlarged photographs of concentration camps on display in the big window of his store for the whole town to see.

We were not Jews, yet we were all outraged. Some thought that we children should not see the pictures, but no one complained. The whole town, young and old, looked at those terrible photographs. I remember my father's holding my hand as we stood before the shop window saying that he wanted his children to know the truth about what the Germans had done. Later, with some of my playmates, I returned again and again to stand in front of the window. We were struck with horror, staring at the mountains of naked, emaciated bodies. The caption said that most of them were Jews. The other pictures, which showed gas chambers, ovens, and pyres of half-burned bones, were no less terrifying. (Ever since I could remember I had been taught the wonderful stories of the Bible in Sunday school and church. Each writer of the stories was a Jew. All the people in the stories were Jews. They were very dear to me. I respected the people of those sacred writings.) We children, three of us Protestant and three Catholic, together remembered that Jesus had also been a Jew. We could not escape from the photographs. We were nine and ten years old.

Later, slowly, quite a few Jews reappeared. I had two Jewish girlfriends at the middle school near Waterloo. One of them whispered in my ear, "Don't tell, but I am Jewish, you know!" I already knew, and the danger had passed. At our new school in Tubize, my favorite French professor, a distinguished young man, was a Jew. We listened in amazement to the Jews' stories of time spent in hiding and of their miraculous escape from "the Nazi vermin," as my father used to say. The years passed. My family immigrated to the United States. My aunt later joined us. My father did not want to live under another invasion. Two were enough for him, he said.

My parents, my sister, and I first met Dr. Marco Nahon, his son Haïm, and his second wife, Suzanne (the sister of his first wife) in the late 1950s. Dr. Nahon was then working under Dr. Joseph B. Wolffe, medical director of the Valley Forge Heart Institute and Fairview General Hospital near Norristown, Pennsylvania, where my family had made a home a few years earlier. Our new Jewish friends from Greece had warm, engaging personalities. It was, indeed, the beginning of a deep and exceptionally rewarding friendship between two families. We had in common the French language and memories of the war. We used to joke that among the eight of us we knew eight languages. We constantly switched from one to another, drawing on at least four, to the bewilderment of some of our listeners.

But the story that the Nahons had to tell was no joking matter. It concerned one of the worst catastrophes that the world has ever known. It told of the most incredible brutality inflicted on human beings by other human beings who thought themselves *über alles*, superior.

Since French was my native language, I offered to translate into English the book that Dr. Nahon had written about his ordeal. Its French title *Birkenau: Le Camp de la Mort*. I had never read, much less translated, anything like it. It was a horrifyingly vivid indictment. I found the translation an agonizing task at first. I was, at that time, a student at Beaver College in Glenside, Pennsylvania.

In the Nahons' apartment in Philadelphia there was a large picture, one of the very few to survive the war years. It showed Sara, Dr. Nahon's beautiful wife, and Estela, their small daughter, both of whom had been massacred by the Germans at Birkenau. Every time I entered the apartment, Sara and Estela looked at me. As they did so, the memory of those terrible photographs in the store window returned to my mind. The images revolted me all over again because now I felt that I knew two of the victims personally, even though I had never met them. I knew a whole family that had actually been in the Holocaust. After each visit I went home, determined to finish the translation and to leave the eventual publication of the book in God's hands.

My family always enjoyed the Nahons' company very much. Together we went to county parks, to Valley Forge, to the beach, to the world's fair, to the ice show, to the movies, and to hear Billy Graham. The best times, though, were the visits and dinners at our respective homes. At such times we especially enjoyed Dr. Nahon's interesting conversation and gentle sense of humor and Mrs. Nahon's sweet and cheerful disposition. Haïm was always kind and witty. He patiently endured teasing from my sister and me. We enjoyed discussing many subjects. At the dinner table one day, Haïm seemed reluctant to agree with my viewpoint. I remember exclaiming, "But all the Jews in the world agree with me on that subject"—I jabbed a finger toward Haïm—"except this one!" He burst out laughing; it was all in friendship and in fun. One day on the subway Haïm and I discussed minorities. We concluded that both of us were certainly members of minorities. After all, I was a Protestant from Belgium and he a survivor of Auschwitz!

Sometimes the somber memories returned. At such moments we all tried to comfort one another. I shall always remember the day that Dr. Nahon with restrained emotion told my father, "Mr. Havaux, I think of you not only as my friend but as my brother." My father and mother were very deeply moved.

Today Dr. Nahon is in his nineties. His mind is clear and his French as fluent as ever. He lives with his son Haïm and Haïm's wife, a lovely Greek woman who grew up in Israel, and their son. Mrs. Suzanne Nahon died several years ago during a visit to Greece. Time and distance have not affected the old friendships.

For me it has been not just a privilege and honor to translate Dr. Marco Nahon's book but a labor of love. I am grateful to Mr. Malcolm M. MacDonald, director of The University of Alabama Press, and to Steven Bowman for their interest in Dr. Nahon's book. I am also grateful to Henri who put the photographs in the front window of his store. He did the right thing. It is a story that civilized people should not be permitted to forget.

Just as my father wanted his children to know the truth, my husband, who is a Presbyterian minister, and I want our son to know what the Nazis did to the Jews.

Jacqueline Havaux Bowers

The Deportation of Jews from Dimotika

# BIRKENAU

## The Camp of Death

BULGARIA

YUGOSLAVIA

*MACEDONIA*

Edirne
Orestias
Demotika
*THRACE* Souflion Rodosto
Ziliahovo. Drama
Seres. Kavalla. Xanthi. Komotini
Dedeagatch

ALBANIA

Salonika.
.Kastoria
Thasos
Katerini.

*EPIRUS*
Ioannina
*THESSALY*
Corfu
Trikala. Larissa
Karditsa. Volos.
Aegean
Sea

Preveza
Lamia.
Mytilini
Thermopylae.
Kephalonia
TURKEY
Thebes. Chalkis

Zakynthos
Athens
*PELOPONNESUS*
Cyclades

**Ionian**
Kalamata.

**Sea**
Rhodes

Crete

Greece

# Introduction:
## The Agony of Greek Jewry
Steven Bowman

The following memoir reports on the experience of a small community on the fringe of Nazi occupation. In so doing, it illustrates the local Christian Greek attitude and contributes to our knowledge of the Germans' behavior during the period of occupation and deportation. It thus increases our awareness of the Holocaust experience in its totality and also reminds us that the innocent victims of the Final Solution were nowhere safe in occupied Europe.

The publication of memoirs dealing with the Holocaust requires no justification. Each witness has his or her own experience which can clarify and complete the historical record in a number of ways. Furthermore, memoirs whose authors came from less-known areas provide often the only memorial to a destroyed community. The present one is being published in English now more than forty-five years since the events described and since the original document's publication immediately after the author's liberation in 1945. Before the millennium is reached, most of the participants in the suffering of the Nazi era will have been released from their nightmares. It is our responsibility to help them record their respective stories for posterity.

The agony of Greek Jewry is a complex story that is little known outside a small diaspora of survivors and a smaller circle of specialists. It is part of the tragic agony of Greece during the period 1941–1944, which still awaits a chronicler. Still, enough is now known to permit us to place the fate of the Greek Jews within a broader framework. It is to be hoped that future students

1

of Greek Jewry will expand upon the impressive legacy of Michael Molho and Joseph Nehama, whose *In Memoriam*, published in Thessalonica in 1948 and now available in Hebrew, Greek, and French, was the first detailed survey of a Holocaust in a single country to be written by historians.

World War II came to Greece in the predawn of October 28, 1940, after Mussolini's ambassador to Athens had delivered an ultimatum to John Metaxas, the Greek prime minister and dictator since 1936. The thundering reply—"OXI" ("NO!")—was subsequently incorporated in the name of the most recently instituted Greek national holiday. The heroism and euphoria of the ensuing five months in the winter of 1940–1941 would sustain the Greek people through three and a half years of occupation by Bulgarians, Germans, and Italians. During these years an internecine civil war was incubated that was to bleed Greece for five more years after liberation.

The valor of Greek Christians and Greek Jews in the mountains of Albania against numerically superior but militarily inferior Italian troops became but one of the reasons for Hitler's decision to delay his planned invasion of Russia in order to secure his Balkan flank. During a short campaign, the Wehrmacht and Nazi troops crossed a disorganized Yugoslavia, charged through the Monastir Gap, and swallowed an undefended Salonika. They then rolled south through Thermopylae, Athens, and the Peloponnesus and finally, in a complex and viciously fought campaign, conquered the island of Crete. From April-May 1941 to October 1944, Greece and her islands played an important role in Hitler's fortress Europe. Greek Christians and Greek Jews were to suffer and resist, starve and fight, and die or survive in fulfillment of the national creed: "ELEUTHERIA H THANATOS" ("Freedom or Death").

Greece was parceled out among the three members of the Iron Axis. Germany took the militarily most strategic areas: Salonika as a main supply depot, a thin strip in eastern Thrace that separated Bulgarian occupied Thrace from neutral Turkey, and most of Crete. Bulgaria received Yugoslavian Macedonia and Greek Thrace in addition to its long-sought outlet to the Aegean albeit one by way of Kavalla. Italy, having already occupied the Dodecanese, which it had governed since World War I, received the Ionian islands, most of mainland Greece, and the northeast corner of Crete. After Italy's surrender in September 1943, the occupied areas came under German control and were maladministered until the evacuation of troops during September-October 1944.

During the conquest of Greece by Germany, individuals had opportunities to escape only in the vanguard or immediate wake of the Greek army and the British Expeditionary Force, both of which were fighting a holding action in retreat from Olympia to Kalamata. Other avenues were blocked, for as Germany advanced south, the Bulgarians followed into Thrace. Turkey, maintaining a cautious neutrality despite severe pressure from both Germany and Britain, had sealed its borders to Greek refugees, though Dr. Nahon mentions a few exceptions to the general rule. Not only did Turkey send back the majority who tried to cross the border, including individuals with family in Istanbul, but the Jews in eastern Thrace were quite aware that Jews had been expelled from areas of Turkish Thrace only a few years earlier. In 1934 David Taraboulous of Dhidhimoteichon (Dimotika) had reported to the Alliance Israélite Universelle the atrocities he heard from Jewish refugees in Adrianople (Edirne). His report mentioned the incidents in Dardanelles, Gallipoli, Kechan, Ouzoum, Kirkler-hi, and Adrianople as well as rumors about other deportations from Louli Bourgas, Tsorlu, Silisri, Baba-Eski, and Rodosto. The reasons for this population transfer in Turkish Thrace are as yet unknown.

After the conquest of Greece and Crete, hopes for escape from Bulgarian occupied Thrace led to or through German occupied Salonika and, for those with special luck, south to the haven of the Italian occupied zone. The exciting escape literature of the British military, which dealt with travel in the other direction via Athos or Thasos to one of the Dodecanese and thence to Turkey, clearly indicates the difficulties surrounding attempts to escape in 1941 and 1942. Most people had neither the opportunity nor the inclination to leave their homes until they were forced to do so. The adventurous, the desperate, and the young fled to the mountains. But escape routes there were not well established until well into 1943, when the resistance began to be organized.

The Jews of Salonika and eastern Thrace might have considered themselves fortunate to be under German occupation. True, they suffered the vicissitudes of occupation, but so did their fellow citizens who were Greek Christians. Perhaps the peasants were somewhat better off; they had direct access to the limited available native-grown food. Throughout Greece during the terrible winter of 1941–1942, the Germans wreaked havoc by stripping the country as thoroughly as army ants or locusts. The effects were exacerbated by the British blockade, by which Britain extended its economic war against Nazi-controlled Europe. The ensuing famine can be compared only to the devastation brought by the plague that Thucydides describes in his history of the Peloponnesian War. In Athens tens of thousands of children and demobilized soldiers died in the streets. In Salonika the numbers were smaller, if only because the city had fewer inhabitants. Not until the spring of 1942 did complex negotiations between the Allies and the

Reich result in a provisioning of Greece. Canadian wheat was brought to Greece on Turkish and Swedish ships under the auspices of the International Red Cross. The famine abated but did not cease.

As bad as the situation was under the Germans and Italians, it compared well with the terror that gripped the Bulgarian zone. Immediately after Bulgaria's occupation of Thrace in 1941, Greek officials were dismissed and Bulgarians appointed to the local administration. The Greek Orthodox rite was replaced by the Bulgarian rite, and there was a concomitant shift in priesthoods. Bulgarian became the official language. At the same time, an exchange of populations was initiated with a ferocity and barbarism unmatched elsewhere in Greece before 1943. A brief rebellion in Kilkis gave the Bulgarian authorities the opportunity for mass executions and wholesale slaughters. Tens of thousands of Greek peasants fled the Bulgarian zone and squatted in Salonika. Tensions there would play havoc from 1943 to 1945. The place of these peasants was taken in Greece by Bulgarian peasants who had been settled in Thrace during the Bulgarian occupation of the area in World War I and by enterprising individuals and families eager to seize opportunities in the newly acquired territories. While the Greek refugees brought the news of terror west, the smell of danger wafted east across the thin line (perhaps one hundred troops, according to Dr. Nahon) of German occupation along the Evros River into heavily armed Turkish Thrace.

The Jews in the Bulgarian zone were not actively persecuted by the occupiers during the initial stages of Bulgarization. True, there was the difficulty of learning or relearning a language and of adjusting to the anti-Jewish legislation that was continually being passed in Old Bulgaria to appease the Nazi allies. Jews also faced the possibility of death by hunger and of roundup for execution by military squads. The Jews of Thrace had confronted these dangers before, during the period from 1911 to 1918, and had known occasional harassment during the early years of Greek occupation. But they had then at least been able to protest to some authority that would seek to moderate local zealots. Now, however, the authorities themselves prompted the persecutions. Thracian Jews kept a low profile and hoped for the best. The Nazis were not yet ready for them.

The Holocaust of Thracian Jews was the first to be experienced by Greek Jewry. Since Thrace was now part of Bulgaria, its story differed from that of the German and Italian occupied zones. The fate of Thracian Jews was the result of a tragic compromise between Adolph Eichmann's Department IVB4 of the Reichsicherheitshauptamt (RSHA) and Alexander Belov, the Bulgarian Kommissar for Jewish affairs. By February 1943, Theodor Danneker, Eichmann's deputy to Bulgaria, had negotiated an agreement whereby twenty thousand Jews from Bulgaria would be deported to labor in the east. Deportation was but a euphemism for the Final Solution; the Jews in question were targeted for extermination at Treblinka.

Bulgaria was divided on the question of its Jews. While some people were willing to accede to the Nazi vision of making Europe Judenrein, few individuals in positions of power were willing to have their Jews more than despoiled or even internally exiled. By 1943, furthermore, a German victory was becoming less likely. Nonetheless, Nazi pressure on Bulgaria to take action with regard to its fifty thousand Jews was increasing at the end of 1942, and there were hints that Bulgarian autonomy was in jeopardy. This pressure in part led Belov to agree in February 1943 to sacrifice twenty thousand Bulgarian Jews to the Nazi Moloch.

But from where were these Jews to be gathered? The

Bulgarians thought they had about fourteen thousand Jews in their newly acquired territories in Yugoslavian Macedonia and Greek Thrace. It was these Jews that Belov had in mind when he signed the agreement with Danneker which condemned men, women, and children to a Bulgarian organized deportation that Germany would transport along with a minimum of food to sustain them during the trip. In the document of agreement, however, Belov crossed out Thrace and Macedonia, indicating that he planned to supply the additional six thousand Jews from Old Bulgaria. This latter scheme was squelched in Sofia.

When the agreement had been signed and forwarded to Eichmann, Danneker went off to a new assignment. The Bulgarian hierarchy proceeded to implement the deportations. In the bitter cold of a March 4 predawn, Jews from eleven towns in Thrace were turned out of their houses, were marched to the local tobacco warehouses (the largest buildings available), and were imprisoned for several days until they could be sent by train to Bulgaria. The figures given by Benjamin Arditti list the Thracian contingent at about four thousand from the following towns:

| | |
|---|---:|
| Seres | 471 |
| Drama | 589 |
| Kavalla | 1,484 |
| Dedeagatch/Alexandroupolis | 42 |
| Xanthi | 526 |
| Gumuldjina/Komotini | 878 |
| Island of Thasos | 16 |
| Stara Shaban | 12 |
| Pravishte | 19 |
| Ziliahovo | 18 |

Frederick Chary adds three from Samothrace to the list.

The official figures cited by the Greek Jewish community of total losses from Thrace during the war are somewhat higher.

| | |
|---|---:|
| Seres | 597 |
| Drama | 1,161 |
| Kavalla | 2,058 |
| Alexandroupolis | 136 |
| Xanthi | 544 |
| Komotini | 791 |

These Jews, comprising nearly all of Thracian Jewry (only 122 Thracian Jews returned to these towns after the war) apart from those who had fled to the Italian zone, those who had hidden, and those in forced labor battalions, were sent to concentration points in Bulgaria at Gorna Dzhumaia and Dupnitsa. There they spent several weeks, receiving occasional assistance from the small local Jewish communities and the Red Cross. On March 18 and 19, they were sent on four trains that ultimately reached Treblinka, where they were killed in primitive gas chambers. According to one of the survivors from the Treblinka Sonderkommando, the Mediterranean delicacies brought by these Thracian Jews ended the famine that had threatened to kill the slaves in the camp.

The Jews of eastern Thrace were to meet a similar fate. First, however, they experienced a series of strange deaths in a foreign land. Since the Jews of Dhidhimoteichon, Souflion, and Orestiás were in a zone of German occupation, their fate was tied to that of Salonika's fifty-five thousand Jews. The dry statistics of Jews in the former area are noteworthy; Dr. Nahon tells their sad story in his memoir. From Dhidhimoteichon 970 Jews were deported, from Souflion 32, and from Orestiás 160. The latter two communities regarded Dhidhimoteichon as their mother city. Indeed, according to Dr. Nahon, all the Jews of Orestiás had been born in Dhidhimoteichon during the 1920s, as had their relatives in Souflion.

The destruction of Salonika Jewry took place in three stages. The first, from April 1941 to July 1942, differed little from the scenario in the rest of Greece. The Jews were not singled out for any special treatment, although Salonika was the seat of Wehrmacht Occupation Forces. True, many Jews were arrested, but so were prominent and wealthy Christians. Some were shot as hostages or in reprisal for the exploits of guerrillas. Perhaps a thousand or more Jews died during the famine of that first winter under occupation. Not until spring would Jews be fed in the soup kitchens established by the Red Cross through the French and Swiss consulates to supplement the soup kitchens previously set up by the Jewish community. The Jews suffered during the first fifteen months of occupation not as Jews but as Greeks. German soldiers sacked Salonika, emptied stores, and paid with worthless scrip. The Jews comprised more than 25 percent of the city's population and owned more than eighteen hundred shops in the center of the city. In addition, many buildings were requisitioned for occupation purposes, including the Jewish hospital. During April and May 1941 the Rosenberg Kommando took the books and manuscripts of a half millennium and shipped them back to Germany, where they would form part of a museum dedicated to the study of the destroyed Jews of Europe.

The second stage began with the forced registration of the male Jewish population on Saturday and Monday, July 11–13, 1942. Perhaps nine thousand Jews were assembled on Plateia Eleutheria (Freedom Square) by the port and in the heart of the Jewish area, where they were exposed to the heat and suffered humiliation and harassment at the hands of sadistic guards. Some fifteen hundred were registered and, during the next twelve months, were summoned seriatim for work in Todt Labor Battalions, now run by Albert Speer, to repair the bridges and roads that the British had demolished during their retreat. Conditions were harsh, food inadequate, discipline brutal, and the environment inhospitable. Hundreds died. More were broken in health and spirit. Some escaped to the mountains, but a few returned from fear that their families and co-workers would be punished in reprisal.

In January 1942 Dr. Zvi Koretz, chief rabbi of Salonika, was brought back from his detention in Vienna, where he had been imprisoned on a charge of anti-German propaganda during the Italo-Greek war. He was made president of the Judenrat by the Germans in December and was offered the opportunity to redeem the slave laborers through an exorbitant payment. The money was raised from contributions by Jews in Salonika and by the wealthy who had escaped to Athens as well as by the sale of the ancient and famous graveyard of his city. The graveyard was turned over to the municipal authorities by the Germans, who had been negotiating for years with the community for areas into which to expand the university.

In January 1943 Eichmann's two emissaries, Alois Brunner and Dieter Wisliceny, arrived in Salonika to orchestrate the Final Solution. Their arrival marks the beginning of the third and final stage of the Holocaust in Salonika and environs and coincides with the deportation of the Thracian Jews in both the Bulgarian and German zones that was described above. During February the community was repeatedly jolted by the progressive introduction and application of the Nuremberg Laws against the Jews and by their confinement in three main ghettoes—Baron Hirsh by the railroad station, Suburb 151, and Hagia Paraskavi—and restriction to other neighborhoods. From mid-March through June 1943, some twenty trains deported roughly forty-eight or fifty thousand Jews to Auschwitz. The transport which left on May 9 included the Jews of Dhidhimoteichon, Orestiás, Souflion, Florina, and Veria. In July the last of the slave laborers were deported. In August the Judenrat was sent to Bergen-Belsen, at that time a holding camp for privileged or protected Jews. The empty ghettoes filled with squatters from Thrace, the emerging urban resistance of Salonika, and the initial British Liaison Mission to northern Greece.

The Jews of the Italian zone were relatively safe from the ravages of the Gestapo, since the Italian forces both defended their sovereignty in Greece and felt antagonistic toward the Germans, who openly contemned their allies. General Carlo Geloso, whom the Abwehr finally recalled to Rome when his allegedly Jewish mistress was charged with introducing female spies into his officer corps, procrastinated each time the Germans demanded Jews. His successor, though a Germanophile, was equally unhelpful. The Germans were not to have a free hand until September 1943, when the Italians relinquished sovereignty over the zone they had occupied. Of the 140,000-man Italian army, most surrendered to the Germans. A few fought bravely in the Ionian islands, but the victorious Germans shot their officers and men (some four thousand on Kephalonia alone). Of those who surrendered, some joined the German army. Others fled to the partisans, now well organized in the mountains of Free Greece. The majority, however, were entrained to forced labor camps in Germany.

Dieter Wisliceny came to Athens on September 20, 1943, and established a Judenrat. On October 7, 1943, SS General and Police Chief Jürgen Stroop, who had destroyed the Warsaw Ghetto the previous spring, ordered Jews to register with the community. Registration was necessary, since Rabbi Barzilai had cleverly destroyed the existing lists before being led by Jewish partisans to refuge in Free Greece, where he propagandized for the major resistance movement EAM/ELAS. Of the eight or ten thousand Jews in Athens (thirty-five hundred Athenians, about four thousand Salonika refugees, and an undetermined number of refugees from other areas), only twelve hundred registered at first. The figure later rose to two thousand. The remainder either hid in Athens in the population of one and a half million or fled to the mountains to take refuge among the villages or to join the resistance armies.

In late March 1944 (on the eve of the Passover), those Jews who had been registered were arrested. They were sent to Auschwitz at the beginning of April. The transport included Jews from the communities of Arta (352), Preveza (272), Patras (twelve families), Chalkis (90), Volos (130), Larissa (255), Trikkala (50), Ioannina (1,860), and Kastoria (763). In June the Jews of Corfu met their fate: eighteen hundred of two thousand were arrested and sent to Auschwitz. More than three hundred Jews of Crete embarked on the *Danae*: their ship sank mysteriously between Thera and Milos somewhere off the coast of Sounion. In July the two thousand Jews of Rhodes and Cos were sent to Auschwitz.

The experiences that Dr. Nahon witnessed and recorded are only part of the horrors to which Greek Jews were subjected. When they arrived at Auschwitz, 85 percent of them were immediately gassed and cremated. Thus, of the approximately fifty-five thousand who were deported, about forty-two thousand never even knew that they had not reached the Kingdom of Krakovia, where the new Jewish reserve was supposedly located. Of the 12,757 selected for labor upon arrival, fewer than 2,000 returned to Greece after the war. Greek Jews were to be found in many camps, where they worked and died alongside Ashkenazi Jews, with whom they could not generally communicate. Among the Greek Jews, men and women alike were subjected to medical experiments at Auschwitz, Majdanek, and other camps.

Three distinctive aspects of the Greek experience warrant special note. One of the early published memoirs from Auschwitz, Olga Lengyel's *Five Chimneys*, praised the bravery of some four hundred young Greek Jews who refused to serve in the crematoria Sonderkommando even under the threat of death. They were immediately killed. During the Warsaw Revolt of August 1944, hundreds, if not thousands, of Greek Jews who had since September 1943 been transported to the ruins of the ghetto to recycle its debris and treasures were able to join forces with the beleaguered Polish forces. These Greek Jews died as free men. And the following month, during the revolt of the crematorium Sonderkommando in Auschwitz, most of the Greek contingent chose to die fighting rather than to be sent to the gas chamber, as obsolete kommandos normally were.

When the survivors of the German nightmare reached Greece in 1945, their accounts of their experiences were not believed. Only the accumulation of stories finally overcame the skepticism of those who had survived the war years within Greece. The publication of this memoir in Greek helped to substantiate the disjointed tales. The experiences of those who had remained in Greece had been quite different, since their environment had been relatively protective, both in the cities among their fellow citizens and in the mountains among free Greeks. Some ten thousand Greek Jews survived the war in Greece. Some other Jews had come to Greece as refugees and had been trapped there by the war, but their number is unknown.

The stories of the survivors have not been systematically recorded, and only a few have been published. The story of the Greek Jews which Molho and Nehama told as fully as possible in 1948 received little scholarly attention in subsequent years. A number of manuscript memoirs show that the survivors who wrote them underwent a psychological catharsis. Many of these documents are worthy of systematic study, if not publication.

The memoir presented in this volume was written by Dr. Nahon in Dachau and Augsburg and was begun the day after the Americans' liberation of the concentration camp. It thus represents an immediate response to two years of slavery and destruction. Dr. Nahon's medical training, which helped him survive, and his university education both contributed to his memoir, which he structured episodically. This memoir is one of the earliest, if not the very first, postwar record to have been written by a survivor of the death camps. Upon his return to Greece, Dr. Nahon gave a copy to Asher Moisis, then head of the reconstituted Jewish Community of Athens, who serialized it in his own Greek translation in the community's periodical *Hestia*. The document thus became one of the first postwar memoirs to be published. This English edition nearly forty-five years later makes available to scholars and readers a text important both for its content and for its historiographic place in the literature. It is Dr. Nahon's personal memorial to the dead Jews of eastern Thrace, whom he had sworn to commemorate during his captivity.

Dr. Nahon was not the only Dhidhimoteichon Jew to survive the war. Dr. Nahon's son Haïm Nahon, with whom he now lives, was transported from Auschwitz to Mauthausen in January 1945. There he was assigned to the subcamps of Melk and later Ebensee, where he was liberated on May 6. He returned to Greece in the middle of August to find his father. Solomon Behar, along with fifteen or twenty other Jews from Dhidhimoteichon, was sent from Auschwitz to Warsaw in the fall of 1943 and was part of the exodus of Greeks to Dachau in the summer of 1944, prior to the August revolt. After the war he resettled in Salonika. Dr. Nahon's good friend Israel Alkabès also survived, as did his three daughters, who had also suffered through Auschwitz.

# 1. The Invasion

Today is April 6, 1941. Mighty Germany has declared war against Greece. War? But this cannot be. Did not Hitler himself categorically proclaim that Germany would take no part in the Italian-Greek conflict? Obviously Herr Hitler doesn't care about one more lie.

Today in our small town of Dhidhimoteichon (Dimotika),* anxiety weighs down upon us. War? Why then, we must certainly expect an invasion of the Germano-Bulgarians across our northern border. During the night all our town officials crossed the border into free Turkey. Only a few police remain in town to maintain order. At about eleven this morning these few will also cross the river Maritsa by boat into Turkey. A good part of the population is soon to follow. Everyone is more or less affected by the fever of departure. Everywhere people leave on foot or by car piled high with luggage of all kinds. Many hurry toward the town of Pythion to catch the train for Istanbul, but the majority prefer the road and rush for a place on the banks of the Maritsa not too far from town where they will be carried safely across into Turkish territory. Christians, Jews, and Moslems are leaving town en masse. Most of the Jews are heading toward Istanbul, where they have relatives and hope to live for the duration of the war. But the tragedy of disillusionment and half truth has just begun. No one knows yet that Turkey will grant refugees only temporary facilities and has no intention of permitting anyone to set-

---

* In the uppermost corner of northeastern Greece, near the Turkish border.

tle permanently on its soil. Upon entering Turkey, almost all of these refugees will therefore be immediately directed to a harbor, usually the port of Tekirdag, on the Sea of Marmara. From there they will be shipped to the Greek island of Mytilini.

The rapid and overwhelming German occupation of Greece and its islands leaves everyone baffled and uncertain what to do. The problem is particularly acute for the Greek-Jewish refugees. The majority have already concentrated at Mytilini, where the Germans will land in a few days. Only a few Jewish families ask permission to cross over into Palestine. Rabbi Alkabès and his family are among them. The rabbi and his family see no point in going to Mytilini, do not want to risk returning to Dimotika across the Greco-Turkish border, and have been refused asylum on Turkish territory. After many delays their determination and persistence will finally save their lives.

The futile struggle for survival is only beginning. Temporary obstinacy or courage preserves life from hour to hour, but no one at this time foresees the tragic destiny of the whole Jewish population of Dimotika, which will later be deported to Germany and killed almost in its entirety.

For four days now, the town has been abandoned. No legal authority remains. At sundown people barricade themselves in their homes. Roving bands of Bulgarian robbers are said to be attacking villages after dark. We hear that tonight they will enter our town. A local security commission has therefore been formed, with the Metropolitan Bishop at its head. This prelate, true to the tradition among the Greek Orthodox clergy of heroism and sacrifice in the face of national peril, goes about the town all day long, unwearied, reviving courage and bolstering everyone's morale. Then one evening at about six, the news spreads like lightning: they are coming.

"They" are the Germans, entering the town in a few military vehicles, like tourists, without firing a single shot. They immediately take possession of the town hall. Their *Kommandant* sees various delegations, including the representatives of different religious groups. The Jewish community is also seen, of course. In a short address the *Kommandant* states that, in occupied territories, the Germans make no distinctions whatever with regard to race or religion. The Jewish delegation leaves, feeling somewhat relieved.

The Germans have been in our town for almost two years now. Generally speaking, the Jews have been harassed relatively little. The German yoke is bearable in spite of the daily visits to Jewish shops, from which the Germans remove goods and fabrics that please them (and at prices pleasing to them), and Jewish homes, where they take the furniture that suits them, and administering frequent whiplashings to the Jews, whom they force into labor gangs to work on a highway. Only Jewish manual labor is being used on this project. In fact, these difficulties are minor details if one considers the immensity of the storm soon to break upon the Jews of Dimotika.

One day my wife, who speaks German rather well, goes with Joseph Alkabès's wife to act as interpreter on a visit to Kommandant Von Kleist. On returning from Mytilini, Mr. Alkabès (who is unrelated to Rabbi Alkabès) found his house occupied by Germans. Mrs. Alkabès plans to ask Von Kleist for permission to reoccupy, with her family, one story of her house. Von Kleist refuses. Then, addressing himself to my wife, he adds, "But why the devil did so many Jews flee before the German advance? Did it ever look as if we wanted to do them the least bit of harm? Would they be so stupid as to think we would?"

Herr Von Kleist, I believe, even today, as I write this account, that you were an intelligent and thoughtful German and, what's more—a phenomenon altogether exceptional during wartime—an inoffensive German. Are you still alive, Von Kleist? Could you tell me now what became of all the Jews of Dimotika who you said had no need to worry? Where are they, my wife, my little girl, my mother, my father, my brother, my sisters, and at least forty other close relatives? The Germans will not molest the Jews indeed! They will make no distinctions with regard to race or religion! Did not their Kommandant offer the word of honor of a German officer? Nevertheless, the Germans have reduced the Jews to smoke, to a handful of ashes thrown into the Vistula.

But this is another story, a terrible story.

# 2. Rumors of Deportation

Early in March 1943, disturbing news arrives from Salonika: the Germans are deporting the Jews. They lock them up in railway cattlecars, as many as seventy or eighty per car, and send them to an unknown destination—to Poland, it is said, but no one knows exactly where. Relatives and friends deliberate. What can be done in the face of this imminent threat? What decision should be made? My friend Vitalis Djivré, living under the impression that he will be protected by his Spanish citizenship, nevertheless speaks with conviction: "We must flee, cross over into Turkey at once, go to Palestine, Egypt—anywhere at all—but leave immediately." I do not know what logic or emotion ruled me at this time, but a few friends and I held a completely different opinion. No matter what happens, I insisted, I am not going to emigrate. They are going to take us away to Germany or Poland? What of that? They will make us work there? If so, I'll work. The war isn't going to last forever, perhaps one or two more years at the most. It is certain that the Allies will be the victors, and once the war is over, we'll go back home.

Yet we receive various warnings. One day when I am in Mr. Assimacopoulos's pharmacy, Mr. Papanastassiou, a professor of the department of German language and studies, comes in and spreads out a German newspaper, the *Donau Zeitung (Danube News)*. Suddenly he says to me, "Do you see this article here? It says that Germany is planning to gather up all the Greek Jews in *Konzentration Läger* (concentration camps)." But what's a concentration camp? Nobody knows. They are, as far as we know, the villages abandoned by the Poles because of war operations. At this time, most of us actually think that the camps will be our future homes, where we will be placed in accordance with the Nazi goal of segregating the Jews.

On another day, Marco Raphael Béhar comes to see us, upset by the news that he has just heard. Mr. Mandjaris, the custom director, has told him of the conversation he had with an officer of the Gestapo. The two are boarding in the same house. Mr. Mandjaris had asked the officer, "What are all the Jews deported from Salonika doing in Poland?" The officer did not hesitate a second: "The deported Jews? Why, they are all being exterminated!"

We, of course, do not believe such information. Surely no one could kill entire populations without any reason. And what would be the sense in carrying them so far away only to kill them? If the Germans really wanted to destroy the Jews, why wouldn't they do so on the spot? Such rumors were undoubtedly the work of agents of the Gestapo interested in breaking down the Jews' morale. It was part of the psychological war being waged against the Jews. In this way people were taken in by illusions and vigilance was lulled to sleep.

The news from Salonika is confusing and contradictory. One day, we hear that the "transports" are being continued regularly; on another day we learn that the transports have been halted. People jump to the conclusion that the Germans do not intend to empty Salonika of its Jewish population. In our ignorance of reality, we choose to believe explanations that suit us.

But will the Jews of Dimotika also be deported? No one knows. Opinions differ; everyone speculates. Whatever the rumors, the most popular hypothesis is that Dimotika, being in the protectorate of Evros, will remain a free zone in which the Germans will not bother the

Jews. As for the Germans, they are absolutely discreet on the subject. A good number of them secretly associate with Jewish families but without referring to the deportation of the Jews. There is one exception, Herr Von Salomon of the Gestapo. Herr Von Salomon has made friends with David Taraboulous, who is fluent in French and German. Von Salomon seems to enjoy his company very much; he goes to see him almost every evening. One day, Taraboulous reports to a small circle of friends his conversation of the night before with Von Salomon. But let's not forget that the latter is an agent of the Gestapo. Why does he make such a point of going to the home of a Jew? Does he not also come to propagate false rumors in the war of nerves? In our times, a German, especially one of the Gestapo, is capable of anything. Therefore, Taraboulous prudently lets Von Salomon do most of the talking during their conversations. One day, Von Salomon announces a piece of bad news: "The Jews of Dimotika will also be deported." He has this information from a reliable source. "The only thing I can do for you, my friend," he adds, "is to let you know one or two days before your arrest." And he continues: "I think that the hardest part for you will be the trip; you will make the journey by railway, in cattlecars, maybe as many as eighty persons to a car. But once you get there you'll not have it as bad as you might imagine. You will lead a hard life, to be sure, but bearable." The next day Taraboulous reports to us this very important conversation. But as always, his listeners draw contradictory conclusions, and we suspect another German plot.

Until the end we were deaf to all of the warnings. Neither the article in the *Donau Zeitung* announcing Germany's formal intention of arresting the Greek Jews, nor the careless admission by an officer of the Gestapo that the deported Jews were all being exterminated, nor even Von Salomon's friendly disclosures would be regarded as indicating the seriousness of the drama in preparation. But does not the human mind find inconceivable the total extermination of an innocent population? In this tragic error lay the main cause, the sole cause, of our perdition.

# 3. The Arrest

Today is May 3, 1943. Last night, Von Salomon told Taraboulous that the Commission for Jewish Affairs and the train for transport of the Jews of Dimotika are on their way from Salonika. The arrest of the Jews is thus imminent. That same evening the commission arrives. The next day, May 4, the head of the commission, an SD (member of the German Security Service) orders all German officers in Dimotika to convene at the Gestapo headquarters. He also invites the Jewish Community Council. He wants, within half an hour, all the male Jews fifteen years of age and over to assemble in the synagogue. "Don't be afraid," he says, "we just want to tell them a few things; besides, it will not take long. Don't bother closing your shops; you'll return to your affairs immediately." He is perfectly polite, almost courteous. Half an hour later, all the Jews, including the high school students, are present at the synagogue. From time to time the German carefully inquires whether everybody is there. When he is sure, he gives the order for the doors of the synagogue to be shut. Then, in a harsh tone of voice, and through an interpreter, he makes a little speech. "From this moment on, you are prisoners. Keep yourselves quiet and well behaved, for whoever attempts an escape will be shot at once by the guards surrounding the synagogue." (At this precise instant, just as in the movies, the outside of the synagogue, which until then had been deserted, is suddenly surrounded by guards.) "You will be sent to Salonika to work there. The food needed for the trip will be provided by your community." (German cynicism! There is no longer a community. Everybody is locked up. The community can do nothing at all, as the Germans know. Yet they express concern as to whether the Jews have or do not have food on the train.) "Each of you will now immediately write a note to your wife, telling her to take along the necessary things and mainly" (here he raises his voice, clearly enunciating every syllable) "all your gold and all your jewels, for where you are going, you will need them. Your wives and children must be in this synagogue one hour from now at the latest."

One hour later, all the Jews of Dimotika, including women and children, young and old, are together in the synagogue. There are approximately 740 of us there. Later in the afternoon, all the Jews of nearby Néa-Orestiás, driven in by trucks, are also assembled in our synagogue.

# 4. The Transport Dimotika-Salonika

Soon after our arrest, the whole Christian population of the town knows that we have been imprisoned. Our Christian fellow townsmen send us fruit and other presents as tokens of their deep sympathy. The mayor, Mr. Eutaxias, sends us several barrels of cheese and loaves of bread in great quantity. The next day, May 5, 1943, soup is prepared for us at noon, also through his care. But the SS officers are in a hurry, as always, and they decide that it is useful for us to be hungry. They order our departure without permitting us to eat.

At about eleven in the morning the convoy starts for the station under heavy guard. Already, our Nazi captors are becoming less polite. They begin to show that they have never ceased to be brutes and barbarians. They find excuses to strike with their sticks. I receive a blow on the head that leaves me dizzy for a few minutes. They start shooting with their automatics inside the synagogue, ostensibly to hurry the slow ones, but in reality to create terror. A well-trained member of the SS—and who can doubt they are not all well trained?—must have no respect either for the beliefs and faith of others or for the sanctuaries.

Every one of us, even the smallest child, is carrying some sort of luggage on his back. In the meantime, and apparently by chance, the Greek Orthodox Metropolitan Bishop, with that great courage of his, crosses the Jewish section. No one mistakes the real reason for his walk. The Jews know that he came to salute them and to assure them of his sympathy. To express their gratitude, and for the last time, several persons kiss his hand.

From this time forward we no longer belong to ourselves. We are slaves—less than slaves, for a slave sometimes has a compassionate master. But what can one expect from the Nazis except the confirmation of their fury to brutalize people until they have been beaten to death?

The train is waiting at the station. As the deported prisoners arrive, they are told to huddle together in the cars. When there are seventy or eighty in one car, the guards bolt the door securely and quickly proceed to the next. My father, who was a little ahead of us on the way down, is pushed on entering the station into one car which is immediately shut behind him. He is carrying the bag containing the family's bread ration for our trip. My wife, my two children, and I are now arriving at the station. We are being shoved into another car. During the three-day journey from Dimotika to Salonika, we will have no bread. But we are fortunate enough to be given some by our fellow townsmen who are traveling with us.

In the different cars life is organized immediately. Everyone settles down as best he can. Most of us remain seated on our luggage. The cars are of course sealed. Light enters only by the small openings for ventilation, one on the right and one on the left, directly beneath the roof. Their location complicates our efforts to empty the chamberpots outside. Whenever the train stops in a station, an SS officer amuses himself by throwing stones through the openings. And in cars crowded with people jammed against each other, the SS always succeeds in hitting someone's head. His impartiality should, however, be recognized. Justice should be done him, for he conscientiously strives not to discriminate: all the cars, in turn, receive their stones.

At every station where we stop, the inhabitants show us their sympathy. Is it the shared hatred for the barbarian Nazis that brings strange people closer? Many of them encourage us by their kind looks and come forward spontaneously to meet our needs, ignoring our SS guards. We are suffering mainly from lack of water, and from everywhere they bring us full buckets. I will never forget the devotion of the police sergeant Lambros Mihalopoulos and his men in the station of Mouriés, where our train stopped for several hours. They went from car to car, inquiring about our needs. For hours and hours they attend to us, going back and forth ceaselessly in order to bring us water, bread, cheese, candles, etc. At nightfall, the Germans guarding the train forbid anybody to approach the cars. If they see a shadow near the train, they shoot. But in spite of the danger, the sergeant and his men creep to our cars under cover of darkness and risk their lives to bring us more water and supplies. In the car next to ours an elderly man feels ill. Someone has a vial of camphorated oil but lacks a syringe for the injection. Albert, the son-in-law of the sick man, knows that I am in the adjoining car and that I carry a syringe. In a low voice, so that the Germans will not hear, he begs a policeman to ask me for the syringe. But at the very moment when the latter is trying to find his way in the dark and to pass on the syringe, Albert, in an imprudent effort to give the policeman some light, strikes a match and holds it through the opening of the car. An immediate crackle from an automatic rifle makes the policeman jump back; he barely escapes. Then, returning the syringe to me, he says, "Here, Doctor, take back your syringe. This imprudence of your friend almost cost me my life."

I think the incident over, but two minutes later I hear from outside the same policeman calling me in a low voice, "Doctor, Doctor, give me your syringe quickly; I'll pass it over to the sick man; I'll warn them up ahead not to light any matches this time."

Tears come to my eyes. Here is a man, I think, whose courage is a credit to his country.

# 5. The Ghetto of Salonika

On Sunday morning May 9, 1943, our transport pulls into the station of Salonika. The train doors are unlocked quickly. *Schnell, schnell* ("quickly, quickly") we are driven in column formation toward the Hirsch quarter, which has been transformed into a Ghetto. Two or three families are put in one room. Food is provided by the community; that is, soup is served at noon and for supper. The synagogue of this quarter has been transformed into a huge office which resembles a bank with numerous clerks and typewriters. All the deported must go there to register and receive serial numbers. Scraps of yellow cloth are being distributed; they are in the shape of a six-pointed star, the Star of David, which every Jew must sew on his outer clothing, above the heart. All the money we have must be exchanged for a check redeemable in zlotys (Polish money). The Germans say that we will need it in Poland. (In Poland, of course, no authority was ever concerned about our checks or zlotys. The Germans fancy that they are displaying their finesse; whereas they are only exhibiting their gross sense of humor).

The Germans never miss a chance to mock the Jews if they can help it, even to their very death. The SS have ordered that a dancing floor be set up in the open air at the corner of Main Street so that the Jewish youth on the way to the Camp of Death can dance. A platform for the band marks the place of rendezvous. With refined sadism the Nazis watch the dancing couples who, in a few days, will be reduced to ashes in the furnaces of Birkenau. And with paternal airs, the SS do not fail to remind those whom, the next morning, the transport will take straight to the crematoria that they must be sure to include in their suitcases their summer clothes, their evening gowns, and their bathing suits, for, as they say, where we are going, our lives will be an eternal holiday.

Many deported persons are taken to a special office where they are minutely searched and relieved of all their gold money. No receipt is given. I saw in that office piles of gold metal such as I had never before seen. The stripping and searching is done exclusively by Jews; at times one even forgets that the Germans exist. But of course, the operation takes place under their control and for their exclusive profit.

Inside the Ghetto, life is regulated by rigid laws and by guns. One must stay at home practically all day long. We are allowed to move about in the streets only at certain hours. We are strictly forbidden, under pain of thrashing and subsequent imprisonment, to go out except during the prescribed hours. It is not that a regular schedule has been established in advance so that we know what to do. No! Everything changes from one minute to the next, according to the pleasure of the Jewish militia of the Ghetto. Everything is regulated and announced by bugles: this bugle announces the time for the distribution of soup, that one means we may go out freely in the streets or must go home at once.

I can hardly grasp what is happening. I keep rubbing my eyes. Could I be dreaming? Or maybe I am reading a book by Zangwill or another Jewish author narrating the life of the Ghettoes in the Middle Ages? Is it possible that, in our age of airplanes, at a time when the radio broadcasts everywhere in the world the ideals of liberty and freedom of thought, people who a short while ago were free and independent are now being ordered into brigades and are being compelled to obey absurd and manifestly repugnant commands? Will I wake up to find out that all this is nothing but a nightmare? No, the facts are there before my eyes; I must face reality, however bitter. The bugles are constantly sounding, piercing our eardrums with their sharp sounds, shattering our last illusions.

# 6. The Transport Salonika-Birkenau

On Monday May 10, 1943, the bugles awaken us at a very early hour. We must prepare to go to the station; today we are leaving for Poland. Our transport of Dimotikans and Orestians consists of 1,070 passengers. The last remaining space is now taken by Salonikans. At the train station, the procedure is the same as in Dimotika. As soon as a freight car has been packed to capacity with people, it is quickly locked up, and immediately the remaining passengers are pushed into the next one. But here the Germans show even more decision and firmness. Officers with guns drawn threaten the crowd constantly. From time to time the air cracks with the sound of pistol shots. We must move on more quickly—schnell, always schnell. Could it be that the favorable outcome of the war depends mainly on whether the Jews are made to move quickly? One cannot help wondering. The transport is led by the agents of the Schupo (German civil police) who are not as rude as the SS. The train stops in a small station. Two Schupos step in and inspect each car in turn. They tell us that all the gold and jewels must be handed over to them at the next station, where a thorough search will take place. Any people caught withholding gold and jewels will be shot on the spot. In all the cars, the prisoners hurriedly gather up their gold and jewels. Some people, preferring not to give their valuables to the Germans, throw them in the fields through the cracks in the planks. Next day, there is another inspection. This time all watches must be handed over. On another day every car must deliver to the Germans ten bars of soap. And the next day they reach our food supply. We must give them our figs and raisins. In this manner, regularly each day, they demand something from us. Naturally we must not argue; we must do as they say without any objection. These bandits, at the same time, operate for their own profit. By plundering the goods and belongings of the Jews, they rob their own government, which, before murdering the Jews, has also proclaimed itself as their heir. The pillage is carried out on such a large scale that there is plenty for every one of them.

Every two days the train stops in some meadow in open country. The car doors are flung open, and the whole transport spreads out in the fields. Men and women attend to their natural needs, side by side, without any embarrassment. Necessity and common misfortune have made them part of one and the same family.

In one of those stopping places in the fields, I come across one of my friends. We hastily exchange our impressions of the tragic trip. "In our car," says my friend, "the situation is horrible. The ventilation windows are not open as in the other cars, they are barred with sheets of steel. The punched holes are so tiny that it is not possible to empty the chamber pots through them. Anyway we try to empty the pots outside through the only accessible openings, through the narrow cracks in the lower part of the doors. But the motion of the train causes us to spill most of the contents inside the car, and the rest stays to form stalactites of feces on the outside and along the doors. The air in the car is nauseating, and the sarcastic SS officers with their contemptuous smiles pester us by constantly repeating, "It's certainly obvious why they call you dirty Jews!"

We are now in a small station in Austria. Our car door half opens; a Schupo is asking for the doctor. "Doctor, a woman is having a baby; she wants you." He leads me to the rear of the convoy and shuts me inside the car where the woman is in labor. She is very young; this is her first child. The car, like all the others, is overcrowded. The delivery takes place in deplorable conditions, in front of everybody—men, women, and children. Fortunately, everything turns out well, and a few hours later a baby boy comes into the world. The new mother's family is very happy and passes candy around. Surely no one realizes that two days later the mother and her baby and more than half of the company will pass through the chimney of a crematorium at Birkenau.

# 7. Arriving at Birkenau

It is May 16, 1943. We have reached the end of our journey. The train stops along a wooden platform. Through the openings of the cars we can see people wearing strange costumes of blue and white stripes. We immediately notice that they are doing nothing voluntarily but are moving and acting on command. At a given time they climb aboard, open the car doors, and—schnell—they grasp us and push us outside. They forbid us to take anything along. All the luggage that made transportation so painful until now, and the food supplies which we so thriftily used (some of us ate little during the trip in order to save some food for our first days in Poland)—everything, absolutely everything, must be abandoned. The people in stripes who speak to us only by signs (they are strictly forbidden to converse with the newcomers) bring our luggage down onto the platform. They line us up five by five, the women on one side, the men on the other. I lose sight of my wife and little girl in the crowd. I will never see them again. They make us march, swiftly as always, before a group of officers. One of them, without uttering a word and with the tip of his forefinger, makes a rapid selection. He is, as we know later on, the *Lagerarzt*, the SS medical doctor of the camp. They call him here the "Angel of Death." (He was, of course, the notorious Dr. Mengele who, eluding every desperate attempt at his capture, remained in hiding for so many years in South America.) He separates the men into two groups: the young and sturdy, who are, according to German conception, the only ones fit for work, and the old, who are, with the children under fifteen, the so-called sick ones unable to work. The latter are immediately loaded on trucks and driven off somewhere. Where? Nobody knows yet. The same procedure is followed with the women. The old and sickly, and the others, although young and in good health but with children under fifteen, are put on trucks; their children go with them. The young women without children are the only ones fit for work; they make a separate group. The groups move on, still in rows of five, the men to the men's Lager, the young women to the women's Lager. We have not yet realized that no one will ever see his family again.

On arriving at the Lager, they take us to a barrack made of planks which is called a *Block*. The Blocks are built in straight lines on both sides of the road. Each one measures about forty by twelve yards. There are no windows; light enters through slits cut out near the roof. This feature of the construction was deliberate. At certain times the occupants of each Block are confined to their own barracks. All doors are safely bolted. Comings and goings in the Lager are prohibited under pain of death. The lockup is known as a *Blocksperre*. As soon as the gong announces a Blocksperre, all the prisoners rush and lock themselves up in their barracks. The sound of the gong has sinister echoes in every heart. What is happening? Are the SS about to stage a mass assassination? It is absolutely impossible to know what is going on outside or in the other Blocks, which are only twenty yards away.

We have, as I mentioned before, no luggage of any kind. The men in stripes have taken it all to the Germans. Shortly after our arrival at the Block we are told to file past a table where a prisoner is sitting. He has been at the camp for quite a while, for he has a rank and is called a *Kapo*.* An SS officer stands behind him. We

* From the Italian *Capo*, "head."

must turn our pockets inside out as the kapo searches each newcomer. He puts everything on the table: coins, hidden watches, wedding rings, fountain pens, pocket knives, etc., even the cigarettes. We are not entitled to have anything in our pockets. The SS officer, as usual, is actually taking no direct interest in the job. He looks on as if he were there just by chance, enjoying the spectacle. When the frisking is over, he takes the spoils away to his superiors.

Now we must file before the *Aufnahme Schreiber*, the scribes, who are responsible for receiving and registering the transport. Each prisoner must fill out a form in which he relinquishes his identity and becomes a mere number. In the German Lager, a person loses individuality at once. As far as I know these serial numbers were tattooed on the forearms only in Auschwitz-Birkenau. I am given the number 122274. My son, who is next, gets number 122275. This tattoo alarms us terribly; it makes the most painful impression. Each one of us now comes to realize in the deepest part of his conscious being, and with a bitter sense of affliction, that from this moment on he is no more than an animal.

At about two o'clock in the afternoon, soup is served for the first time: a quart of water with a few bits of potatoes and rutabaga swimming in it. There are no spoons. We drink out of the mess tin, but as there are not enough tins, we must wait for an empty one. Those who are eating are continuously admonished by the *Vorarbeiter* (work supervisors)—schnell, schnell—to swallow their soup, although it is still boiling hot, so that the tins can be passed on to other prisioners. We have of course no time to wash the tins and no way of doing so. The same dirty tin must be used by six or seven different prisoners.

After our meal Léon Yahiel, a veteran among the Lager inmates, addresses us. He has been here for two or three months and holds a post. He gives us this little speech: "My friends, here you must forget Salonika" (at this time most of the prisoners are Jews from Salonika), "forget your families, your wives, your children. You must live only for yourselves and try to last as long as possible." At these words our spirits plunge into grief and despair. Forget about our families? But will we never see them again? The hint is unmistakable. Our minds are confused; is Yahiel, whether he wills it or not, possibly being paid and instructed by the Germans to wear us down? That must be it, for it is not possible that we should never be reunited with our families or even see them again. Our families taken away from us forever? No, it is humanly not conceivable that we should pay such a penalty without having done anything to deserve it, without any provocation. What miserable wretches we prisoners are! We have no idea that while we entertain these thoughts, our wives, our children, our mothers and our fathers have already ceased to exist. They arrived at Auschwitz this morning, healthy and full of life. They have now been reduced to smoke and ashes.

# 8. The Uniforms

On the afternoon of the first day, the disinfection process begins. Again in rows of five, we are taken to the showers. In the adjoining room, we are shorn with razors and scissors. Next we are stripped. Everybody's clothes are jumbled together and piled up in a huge heap. Any attempt to recover our respective garments is out of the question. Besides, it does not matter anymore. After our shower, we receive our new costume, the ignoble and ridiculous camp uniform. One person is issued a very short jacket with a pair of immense trailing trousers. Another is given worn-out trousers that are badly torn. Almost all lack buttons. On the back of the coats is a huge red cross, and beside it a large square of material has been replaced by a piece of blue-and white-striped cloth. Across the chest is a band of white linen on which our matriculation number will be inscribed. In the right corner of this band is a red, green, or black triangle, the color indicating whether one is in the camp for political or common-law offenses or for sabotage. For the Jews there is a Star of David in red and yellow. On the triangles is a capital letter to differentiate the nationalities: G for the Greek, F for the French, R for the Russians, etc. Special punishment is indicated by additional red stripes and red circles on the back and on the front. From top to bottom on the side of the trousers is a wide painted band. Above the right knee is another numbered band and the colored triangle with the nationality letter.

The German love of uniforms and rank decorations extends even into the concentration camps, but in a contemptible way. On emerging from the disinfection chamber, disfigured in this manner, the prisoners are already unrecognizable. They all look as if they had just been made into scandalous and ridiculous generals. After arriving at the concentration camp in the morning with luggage, clothes, bedding, kitchen utensils, food, etc., we find ourselves by evening robbed of everything, stripped to actual nakedness, and completely destitute. All our possessions now consist of six pieces of clothing distributed in the disinfection room, our only riches: the shirt, the underwear, the jacket, the trousers, the shoes, and the *Mütze* (a cap). We have no undershirt, no socks, no handerchief, no towel. When a prisoner washes, he uses either his shirt or his cap to dry himself.

The most important piece of the outfit is the Mütze; it has a great many uses. First, it is important as the tangible symbol of our bondage. When an SS man is coming our way, we must promptly take it off: "Mütze ab!" If one does not doff the Mütze for an SS officer, from either negligence or forgetfulness, one is liable to be beaten to death. An SS officer never returns the salute, of course. In the Lager, everything starts with the command "Mütze ab!" ("Cap off") and "Mütze auf!" ("Cap on"). Eventually it seems to us that, if the cap did not exist, it would be absolutely necessary to invent it so that we could do "Mütze ab" and "Mütze auf." For hours, when we are not working, of course, and are supposedly enjoying a rest, the Kapos and *Blockältester* (prisoners with seniority who have been assigned to positions of authority over other fellow prisoners) line us up for "Mütze ab" and "Mütze auf" practice. The Mütze of course also serves as headdress, as towel, and very often even as an ever-ready platter when boiled potatoes, for instance, are being distributed.

# 9. The Food Rations

After our shower we return to our Block, where they are serving the food rations for the day: ten ounces of bread and a small piece of salami (often replaced either by one ounce of margarine, half of which the *Stubendienst*, cleanup supervisors, are sure to have stolen, or by a spoonful of marmalade). During our two years at the Lager, there will be no variations in this diet. In the morning we get our coffee, a brownish and tasteless mixture with almost never any sugar; at noon, always our same soup: a quart of water with a few carrots or more often some rutabaga, very seldom some hulled barley, and, even more seldom, a few green peas. In the evening, we get some bread and, depending on the day, the piece of salami, the margarine, the jam, or a small piece of foul skim cheese. Once in a while, we are given milk instead of coffee, ersatz milk that is totally skimmed and sour. The next day, of course, everyone has diarrhea. The small piece of meat to which we are apparently entitled from time to time is stolen at the kitchen by the privileged, or *proeminenten*, Kapos and Blockältester. Twice a week they give us some extra bread and salami; this is called the *Zulage*, or bonus. These few things constitute the meager food supply of the Lager.

As time goes by, one even forgets that people see a variety of foods in everyday free life, that there are foods as different as meat, fish, vegetables, fruits, pastry, and even plain beans. The inadequate diet explains the frequent and rapidly progressing cases of vitamin deficiency, scurvy, cachectic edema (a swollen, puffy condition common to malnutrition), and physiological miseries ending almost always in death.

Such a diet is undoubtedly one of the forms of execution scientifically studied and systematically exercised by the commanding officers of the German Lagers. Moreover, they do not even give the Jewish prisoners time to reach the extreme state of debilitating cachexia, for as soon as they start to degenerate, they are taken in a "selection" group and are sent to the crematorium.

# 10. The Bucks

Our bunk beds, or *Bucks*, are constructed of movable, unsteady, and unpainted boards placed widthwise, unnailed, so as to form three levels to a unit. Since they are loose and slide easily, very often the occupants of the top bunk suddenly fall to the second level or even to the first, the boards having shifted out of place. Each level can hold six prisoners if they all sleep one pressed tightly against the other. But depending on the number of prisoners in the Block, eight, nine, or more are crowded together on one tier. There are no mattresses, no straw; we sleep on bare wood. Each inmate is issued a thin blanket. It is impossible to sit up in our Bucks; there is not enough vertical space between them. We take the evening meal in bed in a semiprone position.

At 4:30 A.M., we wake to the resounding shouts and fearful clamors of *Aufstehen* (on your feet). To render this roaring more effective, it is usually accompanied by stunning blows struck mercilessly in all directions but preferably on the head. *Schnell*! We must rush outside and line up in rows of five in front of the Block, at the *Apellplatz* (roll-call area). Should we fail to do so quickly enough, blows rain down on our heads. Then, once the ranks have been formed, we may remain waiting for an hour or more. At the command *Eintreten* ("get in line"), one obeys at once, even if he must thereafter wait and wait there for hours. The flogging experience teaches everyone this essential principle of the Lagers.

# 11. The First Torments

We have been at Birkenau for a week already. I was a workman for the first three days only. As a doctor,* I am now assigned to stay at our Block in the daytime for the chores. This post gives me a chance to get acquainted with the personnel of the Block.

During the night, no one is allowed to leave the Block for any reason, and inside the Block there are no latrines. We are free to go to the lavatory till the night gong calls us inside. But as soon as the gong is heard, the doors of the Block are shut and we must wait until morning.

In the middle of the night I wake up with a start. Wild screams of despair are heard coming from the hall.

"Doctor, doctor, get up, hurry, they are killing me." It is my brother-in-law Salomon, also one of my bedmates, who sleeps all squeezed against the wall. I jump out of bed and rush on to the hall, where Montag, the night watchman, or *Nachtwache*, is beating my brother-in-law mercilessly.

"I beg of you, Montag, he's had enough; have mercy, he's my brother-in-law."

"But Doctor, you don't know what he's done. It's awful. I noticed last night that someone had pissed against the wall. I could not imagine who it was, but tonight I kept watch and caught him: it is he; he did it again tonight." And Montag continues the slapping while Salomon keeps denying and protesting energetically, "No, I did not, it isn't true."

---

* *Pfleger* ("nurse") was the highest title that could be given to a prisoner who was a medical doctor in the camp administration.

Finally I persuade Montag to leave him alone. Then returning to my brother-in-law, I ask, "Salomon, what's with you? Are you so childish as to do a thing like that? Don't you know that here they kill you for less than that? Why did you do it?" "Now listen to me," says he, "I did not urinate, but last night and also tonight, I had a terrible stomachache and a colic; they became unbearable and I had to go near the wall. I could not help it. Besides, it seems to me that it is a process somewhat less repugnant than to do it in the soup tins as so many others do."

One day as we are out laboring, we see an SS officer approaching. It's the *Kommandoführer*, or chief of the work detail. Even before he is within sight of our group, the Kapos and Vorarbeiter have redoubled their zeal. They accelerate the work, "Arbeiten, schnell, schnell," and the blows fall heavy and strong. The Kommandoführer soon joins in with his own whacking. The job consists essentially in digging.

Birkenau is one of the Lagers dependent on Auschwitz, which is about two miles distant. Scattered all around are the other Lagers: Yawischowitz, Yanina, Yavorzna, etc.* There are coal mines in some of them; in others, factories. At Birkenau there is nothing, and yet it is one of the most important camps in all of Germany if one bears in mind the Nazi conception of the New European Order. It fully justifies its existence and the purposes for which it was created: it is the great Extermination Camp of Hitler's Germany. First and foremost, a premeditated, calculated, systematic extermination of all the Jews, then, on a smaller scale, the extermination of those Aryans whom the Nazis consider their enemies and want to eliminate easily and quietly, far from towns and cities where mass executions could

* There were thirty-nine subcamps in the Auschwitz complex.

not take place unnoticed but would fill the population with horror. At Birkenau all this macabre business is conducted in complete silence. Not a sound, not a sob, not a sigh, not a trace of blood. Absolute secrecy is guaranteed. Birkenau is a monstrous factory conceived by Nazi brains to trap living people, annihilate them, and make them vanish in smoke sent up the chimney. Too often, unfortunately, the infernal mill is working full time, full power. About fifteen thousand unfortunate victims vanish from the face of the earth every day.

# 12. The Lagers of Birkenau

Birkenau itself is a group of separate camps, each of which is designated by a letter of the alphabet: Lager A, Lager B, Lager C, etc. There are two Lagers for women, or *Frauenläger*. The construction of numerous other Lagers is planned. For whom are they going to build all those new Lagers? What future victims on their way to the crematoria are they going to lodge there temporarily? Surely, the camps will not be built for Jews, since the extermination of the Jews, which Hitler holds in his power, is rapidly progressing and has almost reached its end. Besides, the present installations at Birkenau have proved sufficient for the slaughter of several million human beings in complete secrecy and silence. And if, as everything seems to indicate, the plans for expansion now being executed provide for extermination on the same scale as that which now occurs at Birkenau, the Nazis must be planning every year to kill additional millions of human beings, probably Aryans this time. The mere thought is enough to make the thinker raving mad.

Lager A is also called *Quarantänelager* ("Quarantine Camp"). Lager B, reserved for Czech-Jewish families, is called *Familienlager* or *Tchechischerlager*. Lager E is occupied by the Gypsies and called *Zigeunerlager*, etc. A broad and deep ditch forming a kind of moat or canal encircles each Lager completely. Behind the ditch, and sustained by posts of concrete, is a high-voltage barbed-wire wall approximately ten feet high. The slightest contact with it brings instant death by electrocution. Every thirty or forty yards apart along the barbed-wire

48

barrier is a watchtower, a small wooden observation platform twelve to sixteen feet from the ground which is reached by a ladder. In each watchtower an SS officer stands guard with a rifle and a machine gun. During the night, hundreds of electric lights, and here and there a red bulb, shine all along the barbed wires. When one forgets reality for a while, and idly dreams, the scene recalls a night at the fair. When a wire is cut, the red light of the corresponding sector goes off. This is the alarm signal for the SS guard at the watchtower. The prisoners are thus certainly well watched; any attempt at escape through the wires either by day or by night is doomed to failure. We cannot help asking ourselves: why all these precautions? Are we so very dangerous to the Germans? And why? We have no idea. Then, gradually but soon, with all of our being, we surrender to the conviction that we shall never leave this place, that we are condemned to death.

There is only one door leading into or out of the Lager. In front of it is a small barrack sheltering the SS control unit. At night, the door is closed, so that all communication between the Lager and the outside is severed. During the day, the door is open, but in front of it stands an SS guard who registers all the prisoners going in and out of the Lager. The exact number of prisoners inside the Lager is known at all times. When the prisoner work details or Kommandos are leaving for work, they form a column five men wide with their Kapo ahead. When they arrive at a few yards from the door the Kapo gives the command "Mütze ab!" (Caps off!) then "Halte!" (Stop!). And while the whole Kommando stops, frozen in position, the Kapo gives his report to the SS officer on duty: "*Häftling* [prisoner] number x" (the Kapo recites his own number) "is taking out so many prisoners to work at such a job in such a place, etc." The SS officer inspects the detail, counts the men, writes down the number, and signals that we may go. Now and then, either from lack of attention or from inexperience, the Kapo makes a mistake in his report. For instance, instead of saying "so many prisoners," he says, "so many men." The SS man brutally sends him back, shouting at him. The Kapo has no choice but to march his Kommando a few yards back and then bring it back again in front of the door and make a new report. If he has the bad luck of not being able to rectify his error, he and his detail may march back and forth in front of the Lager door five times, ten times, and sometimes more. Never will an SS officer condescend to indicate in what way the report doesn't conform with the rules. The S.S. officers find intimate and cynical joy in torturing the prisoners at every opportunity. Could an SS officer ever show the least bit of pity? It may snow. Our feet, hands, and ears may be frozen stiff. It makes no difference. Before passing that Lager door, all Mütze must come down, and the report must be perfect.

# 13. The Work

The day after our arrival, we are taken out to work. Our Kommando must level off the main passageway of the camp. Upon reaching the yard, every prisoner removes his coat and puts it on backward. The coat thus buttons down the back. Then, taking the lower part of his coat, he brings it up to form on his stomach a deep pocket which he fills up with material to carry: dirt, sand, mud, or stones. All day long the prisoners go back and forth, five by five in a column, for a distance of five hundred to eight hundred yards. Always, of course, we are told to move schnell, schnell. The Vorarbeiter does not let you out of his sight for a second. When it comes to administering blows, his art, skill, and efficiency are remarkable. One single wheelbarrow could do the job of ten men, but in this camp there are no wheelbarrows. It would be utter nonsense to have them. Would it be logical to make the prisoners' jobs easier when the main purpose is precisely to kill them at the task?

All of a sudden, at a distance of about five hundred yards, we can see several of our fellow workers running in confusion. They are spreading out quickly in all directions, all seized with terror. Some run and hide behind the nearest barracks. The less fortunate are already stretched out on the ground. What is going on? We soon find out. An SS officer approaches. Armed with a shovel handle, he strikes everyone within reach, both those carrying ground to the yard and those coming back empty from the opposite direction. My son and my nephew happen to be in the same line as I. As the SS officer approaches, I call to them to run, fast, out of his range. But the SS, raising his club, reaches my nephew and hits him on the head, making a wide cut in the skull. That day, the German leaves fifteen wounded men lying on the ground. Later we must take them to the hospital.

# 14. Sterilization

It is now dark in the barracks. I have just swallowed my meal and am getting ready for the only pleasant aspect of our camp life: going to bed. Suddenly we hear a piercing whistle. Instant and dreadful silence descends upon the barracks. We have already learned that the Block superior is the only one with a whistle and that, when the Blockältester gives orders, he knows how to see that they are carried out. In his hand he keeps a terrible leather whip, his *Dolmetscher*, or interpreter, which speaks everyone's language, dealing violent blows indiscriminately in all directions. Furthermore, we keep quiet because we don't want to experience the "twenty-five." For this form of punishment, they grab the unfortunate and shove him head first inside a brick stove so that his legs hang outside. Then they give him twenty-five vigorously applied lashes on the seat. In time the miserable wretch's screams die out within the stove.

In a deathly silence, the Blockältester announces, "We want two young fellows of sixteen to come forward." After writing down their numbers he asks for two boys of seventeen, then two of eighteen, etc., until he has compiled a list of fifty young men. Nobody knows what is happening. These boys form a special Kommando, "The Kommando of the Fifty." For a while they receive relatively light duties. Then one day, two weeks or so later, they are taken to a laboratory where an electric current is passed through the genital organs: they are sterilized. From that day onward the Kommando of the Fifty is called "The Kommando of the Sterilized." Later, a large number of these young men are transferred to

Auschwitz, where they undergo surgery. During the first operation one testicle is removed; a month later, the second one also. In this way German scholars perform their experiments. In a similar fashion they proceed with the sterilization and castration of young women. While it is common knowledge that in some countries there are people very much opposed to the vivisection of animals, in Nazi Germany, monstrous experimentation on human beings is quite legitimate. But then, a German Herr Doktor will probably boast openly tomorrow about the results of the experiments attempted on people of both sexes who have supposedly been condemned to death and who are in reality totally ignorant of the reason why they are being kept prisoners in a German Lager.

# 15. Music in the Camp

Every morning at six, most of the Kommandos leave the Lager for work. This, with the evening roll call, is the most solemn time of the day. A dozen officers, including noncommissioned officers and a few officers of the SS, assemble in front of the Lager door to count all of the prisoners in the departing Kommandos. The captives are marching to the music. The Kapos and SS officers see that they all march in step and in line. They make themselves hoarse by shouting, "Links, links!" ("Left, left!"). And woe to the one who puts forth his right foot instead of his left! He is lucky to escape with an avalanche of blows.

As paradoxical as it may seem, in the hell of Birkenau there is a band—and what a band! The players include several virtuosos who used to delight audiences in the great concert halls of Europe. Every morning the Kommandos on their way out march to the cadence of the band. In the evening, they come back to the sound of music also. Great music to ensure great marching! No matter how inclement the weather, whether there is wind, rain, snow, or thunder, nothing can stop the music at the Lager. But for us prisoners, there is nothing more sinister and more cynical. Everyone is aware that, while the band is playing its liveliest marches, only a few hundred yards away in the crematoria whose huge, smoking chimneys we see, and in the deep ditches that were specially dug and from which immense flames are visible through the foliage of the nearby forest, thousands upon thousands of innocent victims are being burned.

Each and every one of us is now absolutely convinced that a day will come when we will also pass through one of the chimneys. Not one among us still nourishes the slightest illusion or retains the least bit of hope of ever emerging from the inferno alive. I remember Isaac Sion of Salonika, who played in the band during the first two or three months of his stay at the Lager. He was "selected" to exchange his trumpet for the chimney of the crematorium. Another young man from Salonika, Stroumza, who was also in the band, is sent off to the "S.K." for having written a piece of paper to his sister in a neighboring Lager. Life in the S.K. is so terribly hard that Stroumza did not last a week.*

*Neither in 1945 when he wrote this memoir nor in the subsequent forty-five years did Dr. Nahon realize that Jacques Stroumza survived Auschwitz and led a productive career in Israel as a lighting engineer and as a volunteer speaker for Yad VaShem. The editor was pleased to meet Stroumza in August 1989 and learn the details of his story.

# 16. The S.K.

At the S.K., or *Strafekommando*, discipline and punishment are inflicted. The unfortunate recruits who are sent there suffer such hardship that they soon lose all notion of reality. After a short time they begin to believe that they alone are prisoners and that their former barrack mates are actually enjoying freedom. A person may be sent to the S.K. for a mere trifle or even for no reason at all. People are recruited at the evening roll call. After the report scribe has made sure that everyone is present, he reads the number of each prisoner who will be sent to the S.K. that evening. The victims step out of the ranks and stand in front of him. One after the other, each patient then lies prone on a special table, with his legs hanging down and his seat well exposed. As an introduction to future S.K. duties, each then receives twenty-five blows on the seat, after which they are led off to the S.K. Block.

Every morning, starting with the four-thirty Aufstehen, the condemned men of the S.K. are chased out of their Block with the whip. They all run outside, naked, to take their cold shower in the courtyard. In winter as well as in summer, no matter how freezing the temperature, they must take a cold shower in the courtyard. Most of the time, the Kapos of the S.K., who were selected for their particular ferocity, manage to strike plenty of blows on the bare bodies.

At the S.K. one has an extra hour of labor a day. The prisoners are forbidden to leave their S.K. Block. Their striped prison garb includes a big circle of red material on the back and chest so that they can easily be spotted from a distance. Prisoners who are sent to the S.K. sometimes come out alive. But the survivors are rare exceptions. As a general rule, people who enter the S.K. die there from the blows and from the cold.

# 17. The Kapos

The Kapos, inmates of rank by virtue of their seniority, are the terror of the prisoners and indeed not without reason, for some of them are cruel and ferocious.

Take the case of my cousin Marco Decalo. He finishes his work half an hour before the evening roll call. Overcome with fatigue, he is rolling a cigarette in a piece of paper from a cement sack. For his tobacco he is using the dried bits of tea leaves from the ersatz tea which occasionally replaces the usual coffee. Anyway, such cigarettes give some of us the illusion that we are smoking. Just then, Alfred the Kapo comes into sight. We call Alfred "Pharaoh" after the king of Egypt who persecuted the Jews at the time of Moses. Seeing Marco with his cigarette, he calls him, "Komm, Komm, so you smoke during roll call, hey? Here, take this: one slap on this side and one on the other." The unfortunate Marco, staggering and dazed, is rolling on the ground. The Kapo orders him to stand up, then renews the blows. The poor devil falls back in the dust. This wicked punishment is repeated a dozen times.

Nearby there is a ditch about ten feet deep and twelve feet wide. At the bottom lies stagnant, pestilential water about two feet deep. A narrow plank serves as a bridge across the moat. Marco Decalo is barely able to stand on his feet, the blows having stunned him so much. But his tormentor has not yet sated his rage; he orders Marco to stand on the narrow plank halfway over the moat. Then, giving him a violent blow on the head, the Kapo knocks him down into the filthy water. The wretched man thrashes around in the mud, uttering desperate laments.

He begs, he pleads for some help. He cannot climb the steep banks of the canal. He slides back at each try. Finally we can throw him a rope, and we are able to pull him out, all drenched and dripping. He then kneels down before Pharaoh, imploring him. But Kapo Alfred is not through yet. Redoubling his efforts, he hits him until at last Marco collapses on the ground, half dead.

# 18. The Black Market

The great majority of the prisoners at Birkenau, those who are working in Kommandos as simple workmen, have neither the time nor the means to devise some way of improving their food ration by taking part in the black market. Those men are in the Lager only to work, to collect blows, to suffer pain and torture every day in a thousand forms, and finally to die.

The black market is the privilege of the upper-class "convicts" called here Proeminenten, mainly the Kapos and the Blockältester. They can be recognized by their striped uniforms, which are made not of plain cotton but usually of *Zellewolle*, or carded wool. Another distinguishing characteristic of the dandies at the Lager is that practically all of them have recently had their hair shaved. They take special care in having it shaved at least twice a week. They want their heads to shine like billiard balls. Who in the world introduced the aristocracy of the camp to the shaven head hairstyle? Could it be the irresistible but vain urge to imitate the German generals whose shaven heads we saw in our newspapers when we were free?

In order to start in the black market one must have barter money, that is, some gold coins, diamonds, or gems. The Kapos and Blockältester find it less difficult to get some than to hide them once they have been gotten. Hiding them is an art. Once hidden, they can be used little by little as the need and opportunity arise.

Some of the Proeminenten who possess a small or even a large fortune bury it somewhere outside the Block in a spot known only to them. They steal off secretly at night to withdraw or add to their capital of gold coins. But this is not the usual procedure. The Kapos prefer another, more practical and safer system with the sole risk that they will lose their entire treasure if the plan fails: they entrust their fortune to the workmen in their Kommandos. The latter hide it on themselves as best they can. From time to time the SS officer standing guard at the door makes a sudden search of each prisoner entering or leaving the Lager. When an SS officer catches a prisoner with either money or food, everything is confiscated. The culprit is immediately favored with innumerable slaps in the face and kicks in the legs. At night after roll call he is sure to be stretched across the special table to receive the twenty-five, the fifty, or the hundred administered on the buttocks and backside with the rubber truncheon. Then he is sent to the S.K. Sometimes a prisoner is caught with an important sum of money. The SS officer shoots him down in cold blood, on the spot, without further ado. In this manner, the Proeminenten to whom the confiscated money and food belong take no chances and run no personal risk. The smuggling system is used widely at Birkenau. All the prisoners have grown so used to it that nobody considers it wrong. No questionable morality or ethics are involved anymore. And those Kapos who have just lost their fortunes along with their confidential businessmen, who were either killed or sent to the S.K., reorganize from scratch, rebuilding their treasure and picking out a new custodian. Of course, all the gold, diamonds, and precious stones, all the treasures circulating in the black market at Birkenau, have only one purpose, that of getting some food to improve the daily rations. However, a Kapo who uses one of his men to hide his hoard for him and to hand it over to him at the Lager door very seldom offers his trustee the least bit of smuggled stuff. In Block 27, I again meet Montag, an old acquaintance.

Montag is the former night watchman who once savagely beat my brother-in-law Salomon. Montag has been promoted to *Oberstubendienst*, a grade directly under the Chief or Block Supervisor. Very soon, I am able to win his sympathy and confidence. As a token of esteem, he makes me his custodian. Every morning he entrusts me with his handkerchief full of gold coins and diamonds and takes it back at night. If an SS officer appeared during the day to make a search, I alone would be shot. Montag's goodwill toward me ends here, however. He would never think of offering me a piece of bread or even a potato paid for with the gold that I risk my life to keep for him. The simple workmen are mere slaves, in the eyes not only of the SS but also of the Kapos and Chiefs.

I am now employed as the *Pfleger*, or hospital attendant, in Block 27, Lager D, at Birkenau. Practically all the prisoners of that Block are Greek Jews from Janina, Corfu, and Athens who were arrested by the Germans during the spring and summer of 1944 after the Italian liquidation by the Allies and who have recently arrived here. The lower-ranking personnel of the Block include myself, the Stubendienst Isidor Sadicario from Salonika, and the Nachtwache Bernard Tzifer from Athens. I am extremely fortunate to have these two men as co-workers. Although he has an athletic build, Isidor has a heart as soft as a child's. I have never known him to be brutal with a prisoner. As for Tzifer, I cannot say that he is an ordinary man. In this hell where all personalities soon become more or less corrupt, he still manages to keep himself perfectly whole and unsmirched, without any apparent effort. His whole person radiates a particular charm. As soon as one gets to know him, one trusts him completely. Along with this attractiveness, he has a remarkable intelligence and fluently speaks several languages: German, French, Greek, etc. The whole Block finds him congenial; the Blockältester, the Schreiber, the Kapos, and all the workmen like him. He and I trust each other like friends; we both sleep in the same bunk, side by side, the only difference being that he, as a night watchman, must sleep during the day. Every noon we wake him up in time for his soup.

In the bunk next to ours, from which only a very narrow passage separates us, and at the top, on the third level, sleep a few Russians. One of them is a Kapo. Today, after eating his soup, and instead of going back to sleep, Tzifer turns to me, saying, "Doctor, I am going to be away for a few minutes; I must go to pick up my shoes, which are being repaired in another Block. But do not, under any circumstance, leave our bunk a single moment. I'll be back soon." Then, only because he cannot do otherwise, wanting me to stay on the alert, he tells me his great secret, which he had withheld until now even though I know he trusts me fully. Each morning, when the Kommandos leave for work, the Russian Kapo on the next bunk gives Tzifer a box of chocolate bars to keep for the day. He has been doing so for some time. Today the box contains twenty-five bars, a whole fortune at the Lager. It is equivalent to several pounds of gold coins. A single chocolate bar can be exchanged for some of everything: cigarettes, salami, potatoes, margarine, etc.

As Tzifer goes away, I sit down in the passage between the two bunks, determined not to move until he returns. But I did not expect the Schreiber to come. This secretary of our Block is a Pole, and in his office he is always in the company of three or four other Poles, lazy characters and regular shirkers who are his protégés. One of them is known as "the Limper."

In some way the Schreiber and his clique of lazy pals have discovered the great secret being kept by the Russian Kapo and Tzifer. In the Schreiber's office the gang has been holding a meeting shrouded in mystery; they are planning to steal the treasure with which Tzifer has been entrusted. And they could never have hoped for a more ideal opportunity: Tzifer is absent from the Block. As for me, it is very simple for the Schreiber to make me leave my post. As I suspected, he is coming my way. Seemingly very concerned, he tells me to follow him to the opposite end of the Block to examine a barrel of lime chloride that has supposedly deteriorated. What can I do but follow him? He is my superior and I must obey him. But feeling ever more certain that the conspiracy is about to materialize, I keep looking back in the direction of our bunks as I head for the door. Suddenly I glimpse the Limper dashing from the narrow passage between the two bunks. I see him disappear into the Schreiber's office. Shortly afterward and after some bluster, the Schreiber lets me go. He returns to his room and I go back to my post near the bunk, all worried. I am positive that the robbery took place. I have neither the courage nor the will to examine the box. A moment later Tzifer reappears and without a word goes directly to his chocolate. Merciful God! Instead of the twenty-five bars there is only one. The thief must have left it behind accidentally in his haste. Choking with despair, Tzifer asks me whether I left the bunk. I tell him the story. I am convinced that the Limper made the theft with the Schreiber's approval. Tzifer strikes his head hysterically with his fists and bursts into tears. I soon weep with him. What are we going to tell the Russian Kapo? Putting all my hope in the esteem that the Schreiber has for Tzifer, I can only advise him to go and talk to the Schreiber. Tzifer should try to make him understand that, if the Kapo learns about the loss of his treasure, he will not hear any excuses and may kill Tzifer. Tzifer's only hope is to implore the Schreiber, to appeal to his emotion, to beg him to give back the chocolate. Tzifer follows my advice but in vain. Naturally, if the Schreiber and his men have managed to steal the chocolate, they are not going to give it back so easily. When Tzifer returns from the Schreiber's office, we start crying again. Tzifer tells me between desperate sobs that he can see only one solution. To escape the fury of the Kapo, who will be back with his Kommando in a short while, he is going to throw himself on the electric barbed wire.

But just then we are joined by Isidor, who during all that time had been away from the Block. He asks why we are so upset. Then, without telling us, he immediately puts into action a plan to discover the thief and recover the stolen goods. First he covertly watches every movement of the Schreiber's gang. He figures out that the Schreiber would never take the risk of hiding the chocolate in his room for fear of the Kapo, who will soon be back. After all, if the Kapo ever learned that the Schreiber was involved with the theft, he would immediately barge into his room like a wild beast and search everywhere. He would most probably find the box, and discovery would mean the end of the Schreiber and his clique. Wasting no time, Isidor casually goes out and waits on the road. And whom would he see walking out of the Block a few minutes later? The Limper with a blanket under his arm. The blanket must of course be full of the chocolate bars which the thief is taking to a safe place in another Block. Isidor lets the thief go a short distance from the Block, then hurries after him. Without any preamble, Isidor orders him to hand over the chocolate hidden under the blanket. The Limper protests and denies knowing anything about any chocolate. "There are only dirty shirts in the blanket," he says. But Isidor gives him no time to finish his speech. With a sharp movement he pulls open the blanket. There are the chocolate bars! He runs back to us, spreads out the blanket, and shows us the chocolate. He has saved our lives. Thankful, happy, overcome with emotion, we both embrace him. But when we count the bars, there are only twenty-three. The Schreiber and his gang have eaten one of them. When the Kapo returns, Tzifer tells him about the tragic episode; he must account for the missing bar. The Kapo decides that the affair had a happy ending after all, thanks to Isidor. Magnanimously, he presents Isidor with a whole chocolate bar. The latter cuts it into small pieces and passes them around. It is my first and only taste of chocolate at the Lager.

# 19. Looking for a Good Kommando

At the camp, as I said before, each group of prisoners working in the same team makes a Kommando, or work detail, under the leadership of a Kapo.

One detail, called Kommando Canada, is always present at the arrival of the transports. Its members must remove the luggage from the newcomers and turn everything over to the SS. This Kommando has the most frequent opportunities for "organizing" and is consequently the richest, hence its name "Canada." (For many Europeans, places and things on the other side of the wide Atlantic symbolize wealth and well-being.) An *Aufnahmekommando*, or Admission Kommando, is responsible for the registration of the new prisoners and for tattooing numbers on their left forearms. The *Sonderkommando*, or Special Kommando, is assigned to the crematoria. A *Planierenkommando*, or Leveling Kommando, has the job of flattening all the road surfaces around the Lagers. There are also many other Kommandos.

There is even a *Scheisse* (shit) *Kommando* at Birkenau. This one, which takes care of emptying the cesspools, is reserved exclusively for young women. Sometimes, from behind the barbed wires, we see the group of girls on the road, harnessed to a full carriage which they are going to empty somewhere far from the camp. At such times a few jokers, unable to resist, jump to attention, salute, and shout, "Attention! Here comes the Scheissekommando!" And in spite of the horror of the situation, the young women cannot help smiling. Even the SS woman who, with her dog, is leading the

Scheissekommando, must make a visible effort to control herself and to remain serious.

In addition to all our torments, very often there is the trouble of finding a good Kommando. Generally speaking, the work is about as hard in all the different Kommandos. Everywhere it is inhuman. Brutality and degradation are the norm. Everywhere blows must fall, and everywhere the work is done without the least bit of comfort in the hope that some day there will be an end other than death.

It is, however, possible to prefer certain Kommandos. A Kommando is valued according to the number of blows received. If one is found to be better than another, each individual will try to join its ranks. The most interesting conversation, when friends can see each other at night, therefore focuses on gleaning information about everybody else's Kommando: "How are things in your outfit? Are the guards full brutes or half brutes?"

At the end of October 1944 we are being sent to the camp of Stutthof in East Prussia.* At this time a friend from Salonika is working in a good Kommando, the *Electrischer Kommando*. My friend, who is anxious to have me reap the benefits of working there, suggests that I be at the corner of a certain Block very early the next morning when the Electrischer Kommando assembles for work. He also advises me to have plenty of courage and not to pay too much attention to the kicks in the legs that the other fellow prisoners give the newcomers in an effort to evict them and thereby to protect their own future in the Kommando. The good reputation of the Electrischer has already spread among the slaves, and a considerable number of them want to work in it. My friend tells me that the work there is relatively easy. This Kommando simply walks around the camp the

* Present-day northern Poland.

whole day, along the barbed wires, to check on them and repair them if necessary. But what's more, and here is the whole advantage, slaves in this Kommando suffer very few blows.

The next day, after enduring plenty of kicks, I manage to remain next to my friend, and the Electrischer Kommando starts off for work. It is mid-November 1944, and a light coat of snow covers the ground. We are marched into a forest inside the camp limits. After walking about one mile, the Kommando stops. On the ground lie many massive tree trunks all covered with snow. Our Kommando is divided into groups of eight prisoners. Each group of men must carry one of the immense trees on their shoulders. By order of the Vorarbeiter, or foreman, the eight men line up according to height, the tallest near the roots, at the thickest and heaviest part, the shortest one at the lighter end, near the branches. Each tree weighs a lot and, with the moisture, is so heavy that we can hardly lift it up to place it on our shoulders. We finally start moving, slowly and carefully, the rough bark and the formidable weight crushing our shoulders. We are wearing only thin shirts and cotton coats. When I bend my back slightly to ease the pain in my shoulder a bit and to catch my breath, the Vorarbeiter immediately whips me across the legs to force me to straighten up and keep going. In this manner we carry the tree to a distance of five hundred yards until we feel as if our shoulder bones are fractured. That day was not my lucky day. The work at the Electrischer Kommando did not consist simply of endless walks along the wires, and I quit that Kommando.

The following day, with a new Kommando, I leave for the banks of the Vistula about two miles from the camp. A barge with the inscription *Danzig* is moving downstream, so we must not be too far from the port of

Danzig.* I realize then that we must be in the famous Polish Corridor where all our calamities began.† (The camp of Stutthof was situated about three hundred miles directly north of Auschwitz, which is about thirty miles west of Krakow in southern Poland.) At a very short distance from the left bank of the river is a brick factory where our Kommando is working today. Along the small embankment are three large barges filled with sand that the men must empty with their shovels. A few of the prisoners have already gone down into the first barge and are unloading large shovelfuls of sand on the bank. Another group pushes the sand over farther, and a third one farther away yet so that the sand does not pile up all at the same place and so that the embankment is cleared for more sand. Along with many other fellow workers I shovel the sand onto the bank. We are all working as fast as we can, since our job is to empty the barge as fast as possible. On the other side of the river, two hundred yards away, an SS officer and his police dog are standing guard. He does not supervise our work directly but is there only to prevent any attempt at escape. After many hours at this backbreaking job, which we are doing conscientiously and with no letup, we find ourselves suddenly confronted with the Kommandoführer. At his approach, although we are all worn out, everyone is galvanized into action. Shovels dig deeper and faster. At this moment, the SS officer stand-

* Present-day Gdansk.

† In early 1939, Hitler declared that Germany needed more *Lebensraum*, or "living space." He demanded that some sections of Poland, specifically the Polish Corridor and the port of Danzig, be given to Germany. Ignoring the warning from the British and French that any move against Poland would mean war, Germany invaded Poland in September 1939.

ing guard from across the river decides that he must make some impression on the Kommandoführer. Although it is impossible for him to see us clearly at such a distance, he starts shouting to attract the Kommandoführer's attention. Then he points to one of the prisoners who, according to him, is not working properly. The prisoner at once receives twenty blows on his seat from the Kommandoführer's rubber truncheon. Elated by his success the SS guard then picks out another prisoner, then myself, and another. We all receive twenty on our rears. Afterward we can be sure that our posteriors will be covered with black bruises for a period of at least twenty days.

# 20. Nazi Pastimes

Today I am assigned to a Kommando working on the railway tracks in the Camp of Stutthof near Danzig. Our job is to push along the tracks, in both directions, freight cars loaded with potatoes, carrots, old scrap iron, etc. Many SS guards armed with heavy clubs are supervising our work on both sides of the cars. With much skill they strike us on the back whenever they have the urge and are constantly shouting *schieben, schieben* ("push, push"). There is a wall of barbed wires at a short distance all along the tracks. On the far side of the fence stand more guards with police dogs. Suddenly one of them calls a prisoner at random, the first one at hand. It could have been I but it was he, poor devil! "Komm, komm," says the Nazi. The prisoner leaves the freight car and approaches the guard. At the same time another SS guard follows the prisoner until all three are by the side of the barbed wire. The guard behind the fence orders the prisoner to stick his head between the wires. At the same time he turns the dog loose to bite the man in the face. Instinctively the man recoils, withdrawing his head. But the SS officer starts kicking him in the legs and, holding him by the neck, makes him bend down again. Again, the dog is released. This time the animal rips a large piece of flesh from the man's cheek. The two SS guards are apparently satisfied. They roar with laughter while the injured man screams with pain and terror. During that scene we, the other prisoners, continue to push the cars to the accompaniment of *schieben, schieben*, with a shower of blows stroking our backs.

As we are at work at the Planierium, leveling off the ground, two SS officers come walking toward us, looking preoccupied as if they were brooding over something. One of them has his hands behind his back and is hiding a big shovel handle. We all foresee some new kind of tragedy. They ask the first workman at hand, "Komm, komm, komm, was machst du hier?" ("Come now, what are you doing here?"). One cannot help wondering whether this voice is the one they normally use. Did these men make the same sounds when they were civilians? Or are they doing their utmost to render their voices more terrible? They set the air reverberating as it would if a wild beast were roaring. Those SS are tormented with suspicion. They confusedly sense that in their suffering some Jews have found refuge in a place where it is difficult to dislodge them. Can an honest member of the SS stand for a Jew to find spiritual consolation from the horrors of this world? Should any Jew be allowed to find repose in the peace of heaven where one day, soon, his soul shall go to dwell? Dirty Jews are so often capable of metaphysical speculations that, with them, strange things may very well be possible. An SS officer must, therefore, chase them, hunt them down, pursue them even to their last retreat. He must crush in them all hope, including hope in the hereafter.

One of the tyrants pulls out his revolver and places its cold barrel on the victim's temple. The other SS guard, the one hiding the shovel handle, is now standing behind the Jew. Without the Jew's noticing, the guard raises the club and strikes him on the head. The victim is now lying on the ground. His tormentors kick him to his feet. The poor devil is staggering and shaking all over, his mind in a daze, his ears buzzing. He opens wide, puzzled eyes, having lost all notion of what is happening and of where he is. The SS tyrants look satisfied. Their conscience is more tranquil. They rate their little trick a complete success. Then, addressing the Jew, "Well, so you went on a little journey in your other world! Tell us what you saw. Were there any Germans around? Of course there were!"

And coming from their own mouths, the assertion satisfies them. They are now certain that they have been able to convince a Jew that in the other world there are Germans, too. Germans of course terrorize and torture the Jews in heaven just as they torture and terrorize the Jews on earth. In this way the Nazis try to stifle the last hope of the suffering Jew, that is, his anticipation of a better life in a better world.

# 21. The Roll Call

Every evening at the return of the Kommandos, there is the roll call. To an SS the roll call is the most important and most ceremonial time at the camp. We are all standing outside in front of the Block. The chief of the Block then gives the command: "Mützen ab!" ("Caps off!") During the entire roll call ceremony all heads must be uncovered. The Blockführer passes before each Block and counts the prisoners. The several Blockführers then give their reports to the Rapportführer. He in turn submits the total number of prisoners to the Lagerführer, or commanding officer of the camp. If one or several prisoners are missing, the roll call begins again, and the escape alarm is sounded. While the siren blows, all the Kapos line up to pursue the missing men. As long as the roll call does not tally exactly with the known number of prisoners, or as long as the escaped convicts are not recovered, we must remain standing in front of the Block. Very often, after a day of arduous work, we feel more dead than alive and can hardly stay on our feet. Nevertheless, we must wait for hours, bareheaded, in the rain or snow at least as often as three or four times a week. I have been told that the roll call is sometimes begun in the evening to end only in the middle of the next day. All night long the prisoners remain standing in the courtyard at the Appellplatz, shivering with cold, tortured by hunger, fainting from exhaustion. In such conditions, the human rag has only one hope left. With all the power of its remaining strength, it wants to die, to end this miserable life.

# 22. The Zigeunerlager at Birkenau

Between Lager D, or *Arbeiterlager* (laborers camp), and Lager F, or *Krankenbau* (hospital), there is Lager E, the *Zigeunerlager*, or camp for Gypsies. For us whose hearts have been broken by the slaughter of our families and dearest kin, the Gypsies personify the happy people of this world. Their general living conditions greatly resemble ours: suppression of all liberty, the prohibition on reading of any kind, and food rations that are almost identical. However, the Gypsies have a tremendous advantage: they live together in families.

We can see them through the barbed wire, the men and women together, the children of all ages running around and playing hide-and-seek. They even have a merry-go-round with wooden horses and carriages. A woman sometimes teaches them songs. We cannot help looking enviously in the direction of the Zigeunerlager and thinking, "How happy those people are. If only we, too, could be, like them, with our wives and children. Obviously they are going to be able to live like that till the end of the war."

For several months, life continues in the Zigeunerlager without any notable incident. Then one day, without warning, we learn that there has been a "transport." The robust young men have been selected and sent off somewhere. A few days later, during the night, we hear car motors running and the heartbreaking clamor of women and children. The next morning, not a sound is heard from the Zigeunerlager. A silence of death prevails. We realize that the camp is now vacant. Some prisoners, not Gypsies, are cleaning up the barracks and taking away the clothes, blankets, and mattresses. During the night, all the Gypsies were thrown into the furnaces.

From time to time our eyes wander involuntarily to the Zigeunerlager. Each time we all ask ourselves: where are they, those noisy and carefree children who, only yesterday, like all the other children throughout the world, were chasing each other and whirling in circles on the merry-go-round? The Germans have reduced them to smoke. And why did the Germans keep them for months in almost bearable living conditions, so that they seemed likely to stay that way till the end of the war? Why all of a sudden did the Germans send them to the crematorium? Mystery! Is a sane mind keen enough to comprehend, to fathom, the murky depths of Nazi philosophy?

# 23. The Nazi Concept of Sports

The Lager has its shirkers. Every morning there is a regular manhunt, cruel, ruthless, and wild, after those who try to avoid going to work. The chiefs of the Blocks rouse the men from their respective barracks by means of the usual wild whipping. Kapos armed with big sticks swing them around and chase the men all over the camp. Pushing them forward, forcing them to move on, they literally sweep them away toward the exit from the Lager where all the Kommandos on their way for work, including all prisoners who cannot justify their presence in the camp, must assemble. Nevertheless, every day some prisoners manage to remain hidden inside the Lager, hoping to avoid, undiscovered, a whole day of hard labor. But beware of the Control! From time to time, SS officers personally search for prisoners evading duty. All those who get caught must first do an hour of sports before being sent to work.

The word "sports" usually conjures up pleasant images. When I say "sports" I see young men playing football in a field or young women playing tennis. I see some people enjoying themselves on horseback or on a bicycle, others swimming or paddling canoes. But the Nazis, who invert all things, have given the word "sports" an entirely different meaning: it is one of their cruelest punishments. I can still see them after a control, about thirty of them, lined up *zu fünf* (always in ranks of five). They are obeying the command of the SS officer who is directing the sports. "Now, run!" They run a few steps. "Now, lie down!" They roll in the dust and mud. Then faster and faster: "Run, lie down, run, lie down!" At their utmost speed, they are running and turning on the ground. This activity lasts for about fifteen minutes and is enough to wear out even the most robust men. Then comes the command "Rise on your toes, half-crouch position, jump forward, keep going, jump higher, jump, jump, faster!" After a few minutes the tortured, undernourished men are exhausted to such an extent that they are absolutely incapable of executing on time the commands of the SS officer. Then the blows rain down again. Their bodies are soon covered all over with wide purple marks. Blood spurts from their faces.

A poor Russian prisoner, short and round, cannot bear any more. He is always last in line. His breathing is hard; he rattles. On him most of the blows must fall, for at the Lager there is no pity. The weak must die, from the gas or from the blows. While the sport continues, Oberleutnant Schwartz, the Lagerführer, appears. He has the reputation of being a "good" Lagerführer. The SS officer soon tells him why these prisoners are doing sports. The young Russian is gasping for breath; he looks as if he is about to give up the ghost. For a moment I have the feeling that Oberleutnant Schwartz is moved and will exclude him from the sports. In fact, he is pointing at the Russian and making a few comments. But how wrong I am! How ignorant of Nazi mentality and sensibility I still am after sixteen months at the Lager. The good Lagerführer has only observed that the Russian is not doing the exercise fast enough. It will apparently be necessary to stimulate the man with additional blows. The SS officer does not have to be told twice. The blows start falling faster. The little Russian fellow finally remains prostrate on the ground, more dead than alive.

One session of such sports leaves traces for weeks— black and blue ecchymosis and burns from the blows and pain in the muscles caused by the violent movements.

# 24. The Zahnekontrolle: Dental Inspection at Echterdingen

A time comes when we are sent to Echterdingen in a transport of six hundred men. We are taken to a section of the airport of Stuttgart in southwestern Germany.

The Lager here, unlike those elsewhere, was not purposely built for prisoners. Our barrack is an airplane hangar isolated from the rest of the airfield by a non-electrified barbed-wire fence in the form of a square. In each corner stands an elevated watchtower with its sentry. Inside the hangar, against the four walls of the vast interior, are several rows of three-level bunks. The open space in the center is so large that the barrack appears empty, although six hundred captives occupy the beds. There is no ceiling; the roof forms a very high vault toward the center of the hangar. It is December 1944, and the cold is intense. In the center of the empty space there is one stove which is lit only at night when the Kommandos return; it is supposed to warm up the men coming back from work in the snow. This stove in no way mitigates the freezing temperature of the place. Whether the stove is lit or not, the cold is exactly the same. But at least we may console ourselves in retrospect. The stove reminds us that, when we are not in captivity, it spreads heat very well. Very shortly after our arrival, the five plagues thin out our transport: unrelieved cold, the usual hunger, lice, typhus, and the inevitable selections. Our transport is indeed afflicted with plagues like those of pharaoh. During the two months of our stay at Echterdingen, our original Transport of six hundred is subjected to two Selections totaling 150 captives who are shipped off to be incinerated in the ovens of a nearby Lager, we know not where. When in January 1945 we leave Echterdingen for Ordruf in Thuringia,* there are scarcely two hundred of us left. All the rest, that is, about 250 men, have died in the interim from enteritis, pneumonia, and typhus.

Inside the larger hangar a special section has been established with a few rows of beds. It is the hospital. Next to it is a small room containing five bunks placed very close to each other. The most serious cases are kept there. Every day we have deaths. As soon as a patient dies, the first thing we must do, after taking down his name and the number tattooed on his left forearm, is to count his gold teeth. When the Lagerführer, a noncommissioned officer, comes to ask for the gold teeth of the dead, we had better be prompt and give them to him, schnell, schnell!

The ablation of the teeth always takes place in the presence of the Lagerführer, who comes for the purpose every four or five days. In the meantime each day all the dead bodies are piled outside in the snow until his next visit. When all the gold teeth have been extracted, we disinfect them, wash them carefully, and deliver them to the Lagerführer perfectly clean.

On one particular occasion, about twenty gold-bearing cadavers have accumulated outside. The Lagerführer comes in. We hurry and bring all the bodies inside the barrack. The chief doctor starts the operation at once. But the pliers, the hammers, and the hachets are powerless today. It is impossible to pry the jaws open. The corpses are no longer flesh but steel. We try cutting open the cheeks to enlarge the mouth but in vain. Our metal tools bend on the frozen flesh. Seeing that all of our efforts are futile, the Lagerführer postpones the extraction until the next morning. In the meantime we must de-

* Now in East Germany.

frost the bodies. All around the stove we set up benches radiating outward like the spokes of a wheel. We place all the bodies on these benches, with the heads as near to the stove as possible. The night watchman, for whom the chief doctor has "organized" a loaf of bread as compensation for the grisly task, is responsible for keeping a good fire going all night and for periodically shifting the heads so that the jaws will be exposed to the heat. The next morning, when the Lagerführer arrives, the operation is fortunately successful.

# 25. The Krankenbau, or Hospital

The hospital of Birkenau is a special Lager consisting of about twenty barracks. It is under the direct supervision of the Lagerarzt, the SS physician of the camp. Judging by the importance of his functions, this Nazi officer must enjoy the absolute confidence of the party's supreme chiefs. Isn't he here as chairman of the "selections" rather than to take care of the sick? Is he not "the great Doktor Thilo," the great doctor who supplies the crematoria, the one who—by order of his criminal government, of course—has on his conscience the slaughter by gas of hundreds of thousands of innocent human beings, or more exactly, of several millions?

The Lagerarzt makes his rounds of the hospital three or four times a week. An atmosphere of anguish, anxiety, fear, and terror prevails. Sometimes it is the head doctor, a captive promoted to the post of chief medical inspector, the terrible Pole Zinckteler, who has mastered the habit of beating the patients and the doctors. He keeps his fist ever ready to plunge itself in the pit of your stomach. As soon as we see him approach, we are terrified; no one breathes freely again until he has departed. Sometimes it is the Lagerarzt himself. His name is carried from mouth to mouth with dreadful anticipation, just as if a natural cataclysm were about to take place: Lagerarzt! Lagerarzt! It means: watch out! beware! danger of death! He is supreme master of this place, he is a god—rather, he is Satan himself. The lives of all of us depend upon his moods and whims. One word or sign from him and we are pulverized. He sends to the gas chambers and the ovens whomever he wishes, according to his freaks and fancy. But why is he coming to the hospital today? Is it just to pester or scare us? Or is he coming to recruit his next victims for the furnaces? A short time later the S.D.G., the Lagerarzt's SS substitute, also comes. Then the Lagerkapo. And so it continues. Alerts and alarms rapidly succeed each other, and while they last, we breathe in anguish. We sweat in unspeakable fear.

The Nazi imagination has devised a very simple way of fighting lice: the patients must wear no clothes; they must be naked. For months, in summer and in winter, they are all completely naked. But once in a while, the Germans launch a more conventional attack against lice. They disinfect.

The first time that I assist in the disinfection of the hospital patients, in the fall of 1943, the whole procedure takes place under frightful and dramatic conditions.

Very early one morning, suddenly, the gong starts clanging urgently and repeatedly. And when the gong sounds the alarm in this manner, the whole hospital knows what it means. It is the "Alle Pfleger eintreten." All the hospital attendants must hurry to the Appellplatz. All the hospital personnel immediately interrupt their work and run to the roll call. The least bit of delay can cost one's life; the SS is capable of shooting you down without any further formality.

On reaching the Platz we find a flat open truck on which rests an enormous vat about ten yards long, two yards wide, and two feet high. It is made of thick metal plates held together by heavy bolts. Its size and bulk suggest that it weighs several thousand pounds. We are being rushed to the Appellplatz precisely in order to lift the tub off the truck. In the presence of an SS officer who is holding a long rubber club in his hand, a Kapo is giving the necessary orders for maneuvering. About thirty slave doctors standing one behind the other on each side are trying to take the vat down. We put our shoulders to the vat, and the Kapo gives the orders to lift. The slave doctors stiffen and strain in one concerted attempt to push the tub forward, but at the first try they cannot even budge it an inch. The SS guard, however, is not holding his rubber club for nothing. At once, and with wild roars, he starts hitting the heads and backs of the Pflegers violently and indiscriminately. This is the only way to compel all of these miserable scoundrels to work, he thinks. After several hours of efforts spurred by the blows, we are all bruised but we finally succeed in placing the tub on the ground.

Very early the next morning, the disinfection begins. The tub is half filled with well water. A few men wearing masks dissolve toxic gases in it. All the patients from the five or six Blocks to be disinfected today are already assembled, naked, in front of their respective Blocks. They have plenty of time to wait their turn, since the tub, although very large, can only hold about forty subjects at a time. After a few minutes' dip, they step out to make room for the next group. Since there is no rag in sight with which to dry their pathetic bodies, those who have just been disinfected are ordered to lie down on the ground in front of the Block, all wet and dripping, a short distance from those not yet disinfected. After all the hospital patients have taken their bath in the same solution, we proceed to disinfect the blankets by dipping them as well in the tub for a few minutes. At nightfall, when a whole hospital sector has been disinfected, the patients who are still alive are at last permitted to go inside the Block and to rest on the disinfected soggy blankets. Those who died in front of the Blocks are then picked up by the *Leichenhalle*, or mortuary. The following days, the disinfection sessions continue for the other Blocks, in the same tub and in the same liquid.

Later on, when they have installed showers at the hospital of Birkenau, the disinfection takes place directly in the *Waschraum*. In cold weather as in warm, the patients go to the washroom Block periodically with only a blanket wrapped around their naked bodies. Those who are too ill to go to the showers by themselves are carried there on the doctors' backs. No matter how serious their case is, all the patients must take a shower on washroom day. Each time, of course, many corpses remain there, lying on the floor. The days after the disinfection, the mortality incidence is frightful. Before taking a bath here, a patient had better make his last will and testament. Even outside the periods of disinfection, the death rate at the hospital is very high. In January or February 1944, we had in Block 12, where I was working as a doctor, 74 deaths in one day in a total of 250 patients.

As in the workers' Lager, each Block at the hospital is also under the direction of a Blockmaster, or Blockältester, with Stubendienst, or servants, and Oberstubendienst, or master servants. These men are not physicians, but they nevertheless give us orders for the simple reason that for the most part they have been at the camp for a longer time. Every morning, the doctors have the job of carrying the barrels of water from the wells, of scrubbing the floor, of washing the windows and the stools, of bringing the tea and noontime soup from the kitchen, and of washing and rinsing the soup vat. When a patient has soiled his blanket because he has had diarrhea, the doctor must sometimes wash it. Therefore, very little time remains for the doctor to practice medicine. Besides, often at night, when we look forward with relief to a little rest at last, the Lagerkapo arrives barking, "Pfleger eintreten," "All the Pfleger are wanted outside." (*Pfleger* means hospital attendants or orderlies. Even though they have M.D. degrees, the doctors at the hospital of Birkenau merit only this name.) The Kapo orders the hospital personnel to dig around the Lager for a couple of hours, during which time they receive the traditional blows. The flower beds laid out in front of the Blocks must look well cared for; after all, flowers and vegetables grow in them. It is of little importance that those who put the seeds in the ground will never see them grow because they themselves have been taken to the furnace.

Very often, we must also help the *Leichenhalle Kommando*, or cadaver squad, load the corpses into the trucks. This job is done in the night. On my first night at the hospital, there were in one of the barracks more than two hundred bodies. As we never know in advance at what time they will arrive, we patiently wait for the trucks. Sometimes they are several hours late, but the Leichenhalle must be sure to be waiting and ready. Our masters like efficiency. At last, two trucks arrive. We must immediately proceed with the job. From that moment onward, everything must be done fast, as always. It is dark, and there is mud. We slip and fall. The Germans keep hitting us profusely; we must go faster anyway. Two of us grab a corpse, I by the feet, my companion by the shoulders, and with a swinging motion and a "one, two, go!" we throw it in the truck. Then we run and grab the next one, "one, two, go!" into the truck. We continue until all the corpses have been loaded. The trucks then roar off into the night. In the dark, many times, I grab pus-filled wounds, abscesses, which burst in my hands, When the work is all done, my hands are covered with pus and blood. I go to bed with stinking hands. There is no water to wash up.

There is an endless movement of the sick in the hospital Blocks; many changes occur all the time. There are *Zugang* and *Abgang*, patients entering and departing almost every day. Some of them keep coming directly from the Labor Camp, from Lager D. Others come from the other Blocks of the hospital. Now and then they arrive in groups of several dozens, or several hundreds, transferred from the hospitals of the more or less distant camps such as Buna, Yavorzna, etc. Patients in the last group are bound for the furnace. They are admitted at the hospital only to await their turn to be sent to the crematorium. The outcoming patients from the hospital are, on the other hand, sent back either to Labor Camp D, when they are considered well again, or to another special ward, or, after a "Selection," directly to the gas chambers.

According to a regulation of prime importance at the hospital, all the new patients must be very carefully and completely shaved. The Lagerarzt has personally ordered this procedure. The face, armpits, pubic area, and buttocks must be shaved. Oh! all the bottoms we inspected! Inspection is compulsory. The patient must present his bottom to the doctor in such a way as to facilitate the inspection: the subject is stripped bare, of course, and must stand upright; then he is ordered to bend over from the waist. With his own hands he must pull apart his buttocks, and strain like someone sitting for a bowel movement. The anus region is in this way well exposed and the doctor is able to proceed with the "Control," or inspection, with perfect ease. Very often, the Lagerarzt himself does the inspecting. He brings along his pair of tweezers. When he discovers a vagrant hair somewhere around the anus region, he plucks it out triumphantly and shows it to the head doctor, holding it in the tip of his tweezers. All personnel in the Block are then favored with an hour of sports.

All sick people being transferred from one Block to

another must first be carefully examined to ascertain that they have been perfectly shaved. If they have not, they must be sent back to their Block to be shaved over again, meticulously, and according to all the rules. One of the most important personalities in the hospital Blocks therefore, is the *Friseur* (the hairdresser or barber). He is the head doctor's right arm. In order to keep his much-coveted job, he must be especially resourceful. He must also "organize" his own set of tools, which is really very rudimentary: some sort of hair clipper, one or two razors, a shaving brush, a small cup, and a little piece of soap.

"Organize" is a sacred word at the Lager. It signifies everything. "To organize" is at the same time to receive as a gift, to barter for goods, or borrow from a friend, and to steal from another. In short, organizing is synonymous with possessing—it hardly matters how. The barber, then, organizes his apparatus. His ingenuity is mainly required for economical use of the soap. With economy in mind, he makes in his little cup one soapsud that is expected to last all day; it will be used for all the patients to be shaved. From time to time he adds a little water to it; in the absence of water, he uses saliva. So that he does not miss any spot, he proceeds methodically: first the face, then the underarms, the pubis, and the bottom. With the same suds and the same brush (which he didn't wash, of course), he passes from one patient's bottom to another patient's face. It is like a chain in which patients are linked from bottom to face: bottom-face, bottom-face, bottom-face.

In normal, ordinary life such hygiene is likely to be judged somewhat severely, even with disgust and horror. Indeed! But at the camp it makes no impression whatever. Of how little importance such details seem to prisoners whose intellectual faculties have been dulled from the privations and the brutality of the environment, people who are constantly treading on the slippery verge of the abyss of death.

Life at the camp requires little intellectual effort. Those prisoners who can afford to do so, who have the means, devote practically all of their mental activity to the problem of organizing—of organizing first and foremost a supplement to their ration. The opportunities for organizing are more frequent and easier at the hospital than in the labor Lager. A considerable number of dead prisoners are removed from every Block every day. The death rate is especially high in Block 12, the Block of the diarrhetic patients, where I am working; in fact it is higher than anywhere else. The Pflegers inherit the bread rations of the dead. With infinite precautions— any kind of traffic is strictly forbidden—we exchange this bread for the potatoes that the prisoners from the Potatokommando manage to filch and hide in the legs of their trousers. One can have a complete supper by organizing a few potatoes, a little margarine, and a cut of salami. The very rich can also afford an onion or some garlic. Organizing is almost always done with the Polish Christian patients, who are allowed to receive parcels from home.

At Block 12, Dr. Goltz from Paris, Dr. Horeau from Cany (Normandy), and I have formed an association. We throw into a common pool whatever each of us can organize during the day. At night, if we have gathered a few things, we take our meal together. In the back of Block 12 there is a very small wooden barrack, the morgue of Birkenau. Yes, as strange as it might seem, at Birkenau, where the deaths and the murders can be counted by the thousands every day, there is, of all things, a morgue. The Lagerführer and the Lagerarzt are very anxious to have everything done exactly according to the rules. The prisoners who have committed suicide by throwing themselves on the highly charged barbed-wire fence and whose bodies the bullets from the SS at the nearby watchtowers have perforated or those whom the SS has shot for any other reason—all of them, all these corpses, are sent to the morgue. There, a few special slave doctors, after having made the autopsy, must write circumstantial reports explaining the cause of death.

From time to time when our day's work is ended, and when we have no additional chores to attend to and no sports, we sit on the ground in front of the morgue and exchange a few words while taking a breath of fresh air. A very short distance away, behind the barbed wire, is a watchtower with an SS guard and his machine gun—as if we needed a reminder to convince us once again that our situation is hopeless! But no one pays attention to this reminder; nothing of the kind can impress us or stir our emotions anymore. The watchtower, the SS, and the barrel of the gun protruding against the sky are simply details of the everyday scenery, elements of a vivid, familiar picture with barracks, barbed wires, and chimneys of the death factories.

At almost all times, two, three, or four bodies lie on the two tables in the morgue. Those tables are of course not of marble or porcelain, as they usually are in a morgue, but of rough boards supported by gnarled tree branches. The bloody corpses are laid directly on the boards, which have little by little become encrusted with the blood of previous corpses, which has left large lacquered plaques here and there. The morgue of Birkenau is, like all other aspects of institutionalized life at the Lager, only a burlesque imitation, a mockery of the reality of free life. But, for our three-doctor association, it is quite a providential refuge. Here we may relax a bit; here we have our evening meal when we have organized something special. After pushing the corpses aside—just enough to make some room—we set down the steaming pot of boiled potatoes almost touching the cadavers, for the table is not very wide. Standing (there are no chairs), the three of us take our meal very quietly, in the company of the dead.

# 26. The Selections

Execution techniques at Birkenau are numerous and varied. On any given day at the hospital some die a so-called natural death, but in reality this death is the end result of the Germans' systematic campaign of total exhaustion, malnutrition, vitamin deprivation, and terminal diarrhea. Others, killed by overzealous Kapos, are brought back dead from the Kommandos. Some, weary of misery, have thrown themselves voluntarily on the electrified barbed wires. A few are hanged for having attempted to escape. Still others who have been shot and killed have their faces completely deformed by the bullets. Others die from the experiments of the S.D.G. (SS assistant to the top physician) by means of intravenous injections of petroleum and phenol* in the veins. The S.D.G. is bored; he evidently amuses himself a little by trying his skill at finding the vein. (I did not personally see the above method of execution being practiced, but I have been told of it by some of the prisoner-doctors who had been at the hospital a longer time than I.)

But above all else, and extending its immense scythe of death over the whole camp, the mass extermination rages in the crematoria. These infernal mills gas, burn up, and consume thousands of people every day. The clientele for the *Cremas* is recruited mainly from the transports. As the trains packed with Jews arrive at Auschwitz from their native countries, the Lagerarzt immediately proceeds with the selections, or triage. About three-quarters of the transport are dispatched di-

---

* A powerful caustic poison.

rectly from the train to the gas chambers. The Lagerarzt keeps only the minimum number of people from each train load to be used directly or indirectly at the colossal task of incinerating sometimes fifteen thousand human beings daily. At this first "selection," the Lagerarzt sends to the furnace all those whom he judges "inept" or unsuitable for hard labor—not only the sick and the disabled but also all those above fifty years of age and under fifteen, the latter together with their mothers. But those who are considered fit for work are not necessarily safe from the gas. Not at all. The Lagerarzt saves the best for later; after two or three months these people will have become living skeletons. At that time the murderous doctor, the Angel of Death, passes through every Block of the camp, including the hospital, of course, and makes what is so euphemistically termed a "selection."

All the Jews from the different Blocks, naked, must quickly file before the Lagerarzt: "Alle Juden eintreten." When he finds them sufficiently starved and skinny, he considers them ripe for the Crema. The Crema, it seems, is a ferocious and voracious beast that greatly resembles the monsters of mythology, a kind of man-made Minotaur that gluts itself on human victims. When the monster is idle because the transports are delayed, causing a temporary slump in the killing business, there are always the reserves. The beast then turns to the captives from the camp. It is not satisfied with the sick and ailing. It wants a definite number of persons to devour, be they invalids or healthy people. To sate its voracious, unquenchable hunger, to keep its monstrous organs in good order, it apparently craves two, three, even four thousand victims at a time. And if the Lagerarzt, the Angel of Death, whom one cannot honestly accuse of lacking zeal, is unable to find the quota among the sick and dying, he must nevertheless make up the difference at any cost. He does so by seizing those close at hand: he sends for healthy workers, the personnel of the Blocks, and even the hospital personnel. I have seen dear ones, relatives and good friends, depart. I myself have helped them climb aboard the trucks taking them to the Crema: my brother-in-law Samil Moise Nahon, my nephew Salomon Eliezer Djivré, Peppo Salomon Azouz, Chapat Bohor Alcabès, Marco Raphael Béhar, and so many, many others. Almost all of them, this I can affirm, went off to their death well aware that they were being taken to the crematorium. They went with great courage, almost with a smile, glad to put an end to an infernal life.

# 27. Nazi Courtesy

The Germans take special care in making the big selections at the Lager coincide with the Jewish religious holidays. If the Jewish believers want to address prayers to their God, so much the better; it is for the Nazis a unique occasion to demonstrate that they are invulnerable and mightier than Jehovah. What is the God of Israel to the Nazis? They mock Him: be it Jehovah's will or not, the Jew shall not escape them. The selections take place in both the men's and women's Blocks. Does not Monster Crema demand a meal of both sexes?

The expeditions to the Crema are usually given transportation, even when the convoy is made up of prisoners taken from the Blocks that are only a half mile away from the furnace. But today, the victims just taken away from the hospital are on their way to the Crema on foot and in fives. All are already naked. The Lagerarzt arrives to preside at the departure. Seeing that they are naked, he pretends to be overcome with pity and orders that each person be given a coat. Then, with paternal solicitude, he says to those whom death will fell in a few minutes and whose bodies will soon be shoved into a fierce fire, "Cover yourselves well, button up the top of your collar, or you'll catch cold!" The extent of Nazi cynicism is indeed staggering.

It is cold, bitterly cold, this morning in November 1943. As on every other day at 4:30 A.M., I am working at the water chore. Suddenly I hear piercing screams coming from the road that leads to the Crema. Then I see one, two, three, eight open trucks packed tight with terror-stricken women and young ladies. They are completely nude, and their screams are probably due to the terrible cold. The Germans show very special consideration for the women. After having forced them to labor and toil reluctantly for two, three, or five months under infernally harsh conditions at exhausting and repugnant jobs, and after having exposed them to vermin and scabies, the Germans send them to the furnace nude and in such conditions as to have them suffer physically from the cold and mentally from the terror of the crematorium. It is certainly not by chance that they are all being sent off without a stitch of clothing. Everything has been plotted and calculated so that they can have no doubt as to their destination. My sister Rachel was in that transport.

Behind each transport en route for the Crema, whether it is a transport of people who have just arrived or a transport of invalids from the camp, and as if bringing up the rear of the procession, there is always a car of the German Red Cross. Why the Red Cross? German mystery and cynicism! The Nazis always succeed in inverting the order of things most sacred. The transports of death are being escorted by the Red Cross, which in the rest of the world is the symbol of hope but which in Nazi Germany serves to camouflage Death. The car with the Red Cross is precisely the one carrying the gas that will be used to exterminate the transport.

# 28. The Cremas and the Sonderkommandos

There are four crematoria at Birkenau. They are designated by numbers: Crematorium 1, Crematorium 2, Crematorium 3, and so forth. The first two were built recently and are the largest, with only one chimney each. Crematoria 3 and 4 are older and smaller but have two chimneys each.

All four are often working at the same time. Two immense trenches have even been dug in which the Germans use big logs to burn the Jews after having gassed them. A huge stock of enormous logs is prepared in advance and is constantly renewed for the purpose. Jews exclusively are used to do the work. Nazi Germany has a practically absolute principle of refusing to use Jewish labor for itself, but according to another absolute law, only Jewish manpower may be directly or indirectly used for the destruction of the Jews. While loading and unloading the log wagons or freight cars, a prisoner often says to himself, half seriously, "This is my log! It'll be used to roast me."

There is always a stock of more than two hundred freight cars of wood ready for the burning of the Jews. This wood, however, is used only in the trenches; the Cremas burn coal. But the trenches, although there for auxiliary service, are often in operation, too. There is so much urgent work to be done in the camp.

When the trenches are operating, the whole Lager becomes saturated with an unbearable stench of burned flesh. The atmosphere is impregnated with it; the odor seems to cling to the clothes and the blankets on the beds. The Lagerarzt himself is annoyed by it and very often has his office sprayed with perfumes before his routine visits to the camp.

The workers at the crematoria, the *Sonderkommando*, or Special Kommando, are all Jews except for some thirty Russians who arrived from Lublin after the Germans evacuated that town. (The same Russians, incidentally, were used for the liquidation of the last Jewish Sonderkommando of Lublin, a concentration camp about one hundred miles southeast of Warsaw.) One part of the Sonderkommando lives inside the crematoria. These people never go out; in a sense they have been buried alive. They are only rarely allowed to communicate with the other prisoners of the Lager. The rest of the Sonder is housed at the Lager in two special Blocks under very strict surveillance. These captives are also forbidden to be in contact with the other prisoners. Near the end of the war, however, shortly before the evacuation of Birkenau, the surveillance slackens considerably, and we are able to converse with the people of the Sonder without too much difficulty. These men and those living inside the Crema quarters reveal many details of operating procedure in the incinerators.

My friend Benardis, a reporter for the Athenian newspapers, lives in Lager D, Barrack 27, the same barrack as I. One day he is all excited because he has recognized among the people of the Sonder one of his old acquaintances from Athens, a well-educated young man from a good family. Like all of us here, the young man has changed so much that he is hardly recognizable. At their second meeting the young man takes the reporter aside and tells him about all his tribulations.

"I knew what passed through your mind when you first saw me," says he, "I could read in your eyes the shocking astonishment, the contempt, the utter disgust even, that my profession of today inspires in you, my profession of body burner. Ah! how far you all are from realizing how much I myself and my buddies from the Sonder are suffering from our situation. We at the Sonder are doubly cursed. But the Nazis are masters when it comes to educating their slaves to achieve the goal that they have fixed in their minds. As soon as I arrived at Birkenau, I was thrown with all our transport in the Quarantine Camp. There was no work at all there and not much food either. We suffered from terrible hunger. Several times a day, we had Eintreten and roll call. No sooner had we returned to the Block than we were again told to Eintreten. We spent the entire day lining up in front of the Block. We were exhausted and collapsed from fatigue. The evening roll call was endless; for more than two hours we stood at attention in the courtyard. At night, we lay down, hoping for a few hours' rest at last. But no! An hour later, we heard strident and imperative blasts of the whistle once again. Shrill and terrible shouts echoed from the Stubendienst: 'Aufstehn! Appell! Schnell! Schnell!'

"We must run to the Appellplatz. We spend one more hour standing in the darkness for no reason other than to wear us out completely. Then we go back to the Block and fall back to sleep. Near the middle of the night we hear the same whistle blasts, the same shouting. 'Get up! Roll call!' Every night the roll call repeats itself two or three times. It is impossible to sleep without interruption. The routine lasts for about a month. Then one day the Lagerarzt pays us a visit. He makes a selection. He chooses the few strongest among us; in some cases he feels our muscles. After the selection we are taken to Lager D and thrown into Barracks 9 to 11, the Sonderkommando barracks. There the situation changes completely. No one ever bothers us any more. There is no more Eintreten. We may lie down on our beds all day long; we are no longer awakened at night; food is substantial and abundant. With each meal we are served a few glasses of Schnapps. This routine continues for a few days, and each time the dosage of Schnapps is increased. But why in the world are we enjoying so many little attentions after a month of fasting? We all wonder. Something fishy must be going on. The Germans have something up their sleeves, and it's going to be bad. In order not to think about it too much, we immerse ourselves in the Schnapps, which is being distributed in greater and greater quantity. The SS men smile as they watch us drink. They encourage us to drink more. Some of them even become friendly and tap us familiarly on the shoulders. 'Gut, ja? Gut?' We drown our thoughts. On the third day, a Kapo shows up. 'Come on, lads,' he says, 'a last little glass, and then we're going to do a little work!' Lined up in fives, half drunk, we are taken somewhere. We approach a brick building flanked by a high chimney. A factory? But why does the deep and oppressive silence of this place arouse in each of us the sinister suspicion that we have all obscured with alcohol and buried in the depths of our minds? Somehow we know instinctively: in this dismal place slaughter is being committed.

"We enter the courtyard, and then we cross the threshold of the building. Above the doorway I read the word *Baden*. Are they taking us to the baths? We are led to a very large room in the basement. Nothing unusual there; at the far end, a door; on the walls, hundreds of numbered hooks to hang clothes on. I am, however, obstinate in trying to locate somewhere a mysterious death-dealing machine. Maybe the ceiling or the walls harbor some ingenious apparatus to destroy people? The Germans are so subtle. But there is nothing at all. This room is like any other room—and yet an unspeakable fear claws at my throat. All of a sudden we hear truck motors outside. Trucks stop in front of the door. Women and children are now entering the room. More come and still more. There must be about three hundred of them. The trucks go away; the door is closed. Several SS guards and a few of the older captives on duty are now moving around the room. They order the women to undress: 'Schnell, schnell! Los, los!' ('fast, fast, go on, go on.') Whips spring into action; pistols gleam. The women must undress quickly. They are instructed to hang their clothes carefully on the hooks and especially to remember their numbers so as to avoid confusion after the baths. Too modest to stand naked in front of so many men, a few women are still wearing their slips. But the men order them to take off everything, 'Alles! alles!' I will never forget the French woman who asked me, begged me, 'Monsieur, ayez soin, je vous prie, de mes effets; les Boches nous ont déjà tout pris; c'est tout ce qu'il me reste.' ('Sir, please take care of my clothes; the Germans have already taken everything from us; this is all I have left').

"How far she was from comprehending what awaited her behind the door! The back door is flung open. All the women and all the children are pushed through the opening, and the door is closed behind them. Again, outside, the roar of trucks and the screech of their brakes. And again, women and children are taken into the huge hall in the same number as before. They receive the same injunctions: 'Take off your clothes, schnell, schnell!' This group is also propelled through the back door. Then new trucks arrive. More and more women and children get off.

"The procedure is repeated five or six times. Then an officer asks, 'How many have there been?' The answer comes: 'Fourteen hundred!' The Kapo orders us, 'Eintreten by five. That's enough work for today.' We go back to the Block. When we reach our barrack, they serve us something to eat. But no one is hungry. No one can touch the food. Our minds are elsewhere. Our thoughts return reluctantly yet insistently to the door at the far end of that building. We all want to penetrate the horrible mystery of the back room. That's where the Crematorium is. We have heard about it for some time. We are convinced that that's where it must be. But how is the job done? What diabolical machine have the Germans invented to kill fourteen hundred persons at a time? And while waiting for Death to deliver them, do these poor people suffer much? How long does the cruel drama last? And what about all of us? Why did they take us there as if we were attending a rehearsal? Just to see the prelude to a fantastic drama? Ah! to be able to obliterate each thought, to see our intelligence sink and leave us, that would be deliverance! We abandon ourselves to the Schnapps, which is being served ever more freely. To drink, to drink always, to imbibe the alcohol until all trace of feeling and consciousness is gone. For two days the new workers of the Sonderkommando eat almost nothing; they ask only for Schnapps. Then comes the Kapo. 'Eintreten by five; we're going to work!' We are taken to the same large hall. The hooks are overloaded with clothes, but this time they are men's clothes. The same officer as the other day asks,

" 'How many are they?'

" 'Two thousand.'

" 'Is everything ready? Can we start?'

" 'Everything's ready.'

"They open the back door. I am getting closer and closer. The door leads to a narrow hallway. On one side is another door, its panels lined with wide strips of thick rubber. This door shuts airtight. Above it is an electric clock and a kind of attic window with very thick glass. An SS officer opens a case and takes out two metal containers very similar to vacuum flasks or thermos bottles; they contain a gas called Cyclone.* He opens the

* Zyklon B, a prussic acid gas used for disinfection and as an in-

small window, hurls the thermos bottles into the room, and shuts the window hastily. What time does the electric clock say? Five past eight! On striking the floor, the thermos bottles break and detonate. Immediately afterward, I hear a second noise. It sounds like tires blowing out, or rather, like the hissing of a hundred snakes.

"There are screams of distress, atrocious shouts and shrieks. They grow louder and louder. Am I in hell? The walls of the gas chamber shake under the incredible impact and the desperate thrashing of those being asphyxiated. Arms and fists smash repeatedly against the thick glass of the small observation window in a last attempt to break it down. All of us are pale. Our hair stands on end. Beads of cold sweat line our foreheads. The blood seems to drain from our bodies. Some of us sway and feel faint. The screaming now seems to be losing intensity. The cries become fewer. They give way to groaning, to a mere wailing, to muffled and far distant laments. Then there is absolute silence. How long did it take? Three minutes, five minutes perhaps? The SS officer looks at the clock. He presses an electric button. Inside the gas chamber, ventilators clear the air. The door is pushed open. What a horrible sight! A mass of dead bodies sprawled on top of each other, their limbs intertwined, their eyes popping out of their sockets, their mouths frothing, their faces pinched, blood, stains. The bodies are turned over, and we must proceed immediately with the Zähnekontrolle, or dental ablation. The gold teeth are extracted and placed in a case. The women's hair is cut off and will soon be sent to Germany. Specially arranged elevators carry to the ovens on the next floor the remains of two thousand human beings who just a short while ago were alive.

"After a few days, the supervisors decide that the

secticide. It was manufactured by Degesch (Deutsche Gesellschaft für Schädlingsbekämpfung).

newly employed men are sufficiently well trained for their work; they stop giving out Schnapps. But for the Sonder people, Schnapps is life itself, and so they buy it from their Kapo in exchange for gold or diamonds. The Kapo himself gets the liquor from the Polish civilians who come every day from their villages to work in the camp. The slaves from the Sonder 'organize' their gold coins, diamonds, gems, and jewels by searching inside the lining of the victims' clothes. This pilfering is done under the eyes of the Germans, and of course the largest part of the take goes to them. The Germans tolerate these 'organizings' tacitly. But one must be extremely skillful and not let himself be caught. When a prisoner is caught carrying gold or jewels, he is shot on the spot.

"There are several labor gangs for the work in the Crema. Some of the workers remove the bodies from the gas chambers and send them up to the ovens on the next floor; others are responsible for cleaning the gas rooms. They must wash and scrub the floors thoroughly after each gassing operation to erase the traces of blood and stains that the poor victims have left in their horrible agony. Some workers labor around the furnaces. Still other special details pulverize the debris of calcined bones with large, heavy wooden mallets. The ashes are picked up, loaded on trucks, and scattered in the river Vistula. After a few hours there remains no material trace of the few thousands who were gassed, not even a particle of bone. It is as if those human beings had never existed.

"The various Kommandos perform their jobs under the direct surveillance of the SS officers, who force their slaves to sing while crushing human bones. Some of the SS, who have perverse natures and are cynics and sadists, amuse themselves by using the end of a burning log to prod the genitals on the women's dead bodies. Do they suffer from some kind of paranoia that they find it necessary to sterilize every Jewish woman, although she is already dead, to prevent the reproduction of the accursed and abhorred Jewish race?

"Sometimes the number of people to be killed is not high enough to justify the use of the gas chamber. Cyclone gas is expensive. When a mere one or two hundred persons must be murdered, the chief of the Crema, Hauptscharführer Moll, shoots them down with his pistol. He can even joke with his victims. 'Say, have you a keen sense of smell? Do you smell this rose?' And he fires directly into the nostril. During this bloodthirsty bandit's tenure at Birkenau, he personally murdered tens of thousands of victims.

"The various incidents that take place in the Crema are exceptional and unique. The people of the newly arrived transports, having no idea of what is in store for them, arrive like sheep at the slaughterhouse. One day, a young woman—very beautiful, they say, an artist—waits with the rest of her transport in the large room adjoining the gas chamber. Like all her female companions, she is already nude except for her underpants. The Rapportführer Schillinger (all of Birkenau knows the Rapportführer Schillinger; he is the most ferocious of bandits) orders her to take off her underpants. She refuses. Schillinger approaches her to pull them off. Then something extraordinary happens: with the speed of lightning, the young woman seizes Schillinger's revolver, which hangs from his waist, and kills the miserable ruffian with a single bullet. That same day the entire Lager learns about Schillinger's death and celebrates a little.*

"Many SS officers believe that they are quite eloquent and fancy themselves great orators. A transport of con-

* A full account appears in Filip Müller, *Eyewitness Auschwitz: Three Years in the Gas Chambers* (New York, 1979), pp. 86–89.

demned prisoners has just arrived at the crematorium. In a few minutes the human cargo will be engulfed in flames. An SS officer wishes to address them with a short speech: 'Over there, far away from home, for months, you have worked hard for the good and the greatness of our country. The grateful fatherland owes you a reward. In this House of Rest erected especially for you, you will be treated like the true heroes that you are.'

"This rhetoric leaves the audience perfectly cold; all the faces are placid. They are hoping for only one thing: to die and die quickly.

"Every five or six months the staff of the Sonderkommando is replaced. The Germans retire the old workmen in the simplest way: the Germans send them also to the furnace. The men of the Sonder know very well what lies in store for them. While throwing hundreds of thousands of corpses into the furnace day and night, and while crushing, without ceasing, the residue of burned human bones, they continuously hum macabre ballads and refrains of their own invention that concern their own ineluctable and imminent fate. Their turn to be burned comes closer with the passage of each day. Their time is running out with mathematical precision. But habit is such that they continue their ghastly work with songs that echo incessantly in their minds, like an obsession."

# 29. The Last Transports

At the end of October 1944, the Germans begin the evacuation of all the camps in the region of Auschwitz. Are they expecting a great Russian offensive? They hastily dispatch a large number of young Jewish women to the furnace. The rest of the Jews, who are being transferred to the different Lagers in Germany, have been granted no special reprieve, however. Nazi minds have long been made up. Himmler is determined to have all the Jews destroyed, starting with all those whom the Germans have in their grip. But foreign manpower must not be involved in the systematic destruction of the Jews; Jews alone must accomplish the annihilation of their own race. And at the time of the evacuation of Birkenau, enough Jews remain scattered in the numerous German camps: other Jews must be used to exterminate them.

I am being sent to a camp near Danzig, Germany—to Stutthof. But the Russians are advancing in that direction also. A few days later we are transferred to the opposite part of Germany, to Echterdingen (Stuttgart), and from there to Ordruf, near Gotha in Thuringia. All these changes are effected under deplorable conditions. Many of the prisoners die from the cold and from physiological miseries. We live exclusively on the snow that we manage to scrape through the cracks in the train cars. On April 3, 1945, we begin the final stage of our tragic odyssey.

For a month now, I have been with Dr. Béja from Salonika at the Lager at Klavinkel. It is a very small camp in a forest about eight miles from Ordruf. I work at the hospital, where there are about sixty patients. Today the

SS forces are preparing to evacuate the camp. All the prisoners receive one loaf of bread each for the transport's journey, whereas the doctors and all the personnel of the hospital are fortunate to get two loaves each, the second loaf representing the ration of the patients who were taken away on trucks just before the bread arrived. The hulled barley soup served at the hospital today was really excellent, thick and rich; the cooks must have used up all their supplies before the evacuation. Each of us gulps down several portions of soup; for once we are all so full that we cannot possibly swallow another morsel till the next day. The prisoners working in the Kommandos are so famished that they have already consumed the bread supposed to last for the entire journey, without caring about the fast days to come.

At about six o'clock in the evening all the Lagers from the region of Ordruf form into transports for unknown destinations. We can hear the mortars distinctly; the battle must not be far off. Some even whisper that the Americans are already in Erfurt and Gotha, only about thirteen miles away. If only they could catch up with us! For the first time since we have been in the tigers' clutches, a spark of hope flickers in our minds. Night soon comes; the darkness is dense and heavy. The transport takes a crossroad, a shortcut through the mountains and forests of Thuringia. It is not a road but rather a path of ruts and furrows; we slog through the mud all night, hustled by the SS officers and harassed by the dogs. The trek continues the next day without any rest. Each step causes painful twitches in the thigh muscles, but we cannot stop to rest and regain some strength. We must march on.

There are many Russian civilian prisoners in our transport. The endurance and perseverance of those people is something extraordinary. Fatigue and exhaustion force most of us to abandon our coats on the road, although we have nothing with which to cover ourselves during the very cold nights that we must spend under the stars. Many of the Russians are carrying huge logs of dry wood on their backs, for dozens of miles, so that we can make a fire when we have the chance to stop and prepare tea—or more exactly, to heat some rather muddy water that we will call tea.

We continue our journey in rows of five, as always. Walking side by side are Dr. Béja, myself, and another Jew from Salonika. Dr. Béja has the flu; he drags himself along, leaning on my arm. He is incapable of carrying any burden and has entrusted his two still untouched loaves of bread to his Salonikan companion. I still have my two whole loaves also. Two rows ahead of us are a few Russians. One of them has apparently noticed the bulging loaves under the thin material of the sacks hanging from our shoulders. With his keen mind he soon devises a plan to steal one of our loaves. We, of course, know nothing about it. The Russian is waiting for the SS officer who is walking back and forth along the moving transport to reach our row. When the latter stands near us, in step with our row, the Russian cries out, "My bread, what happened to my bread? They have stolen my bread!" For a few seconds he pretends to be looking around for the thief, and then he resolutely walks toward the Salonikan, whom he must have chosen in advance, feels his sack up and down, and discovers the "stolen" bread in it. "I found it," he exclaims. "Here is my bread!" The SS guard, who has followed this scenario with interest, approaches the Salonikan. The Russian seizes the unique opportunity to unveil his irresistible argument: "He stole my bread; he is a Jew!" Nothing could be more persuasive. The Salonikan immediately receives numerous blows from the German's rifle. The SS officer takes one loaf out of the sack and hands it to the Russian. The latter grabs it, runs back to his place a few rows in front of us, and disappears, devouring his booty as fast as he can.

A few steps ahead of me I see a prisoner collapse by the roadside, completely exhausted. His face is livid. It is easy to see that he cannot walk another step. An SS guard who has also seen him approaches and stands before him. Very quietly, he takes his rifle from his shoulder strap, places the barrel a few inches from the poor devil's head, and shoots. He executes the maneuvers mechanically, as if they were simply practice exercises. The poor man dies instantaneously, without even uttering a sigh.

At Birkenau, I saw mountains of dead bodies. I personally witnessed the departure of thousands upon thousands of people for the gas chambers. At the time of this transport I believe myself no longer sensitive to the sight of torture and brutality, but that murder committed there, before my eyes so methodically and so coldly, shocks and shakes me very badly. Later that day and on the following days, quick executions of this kind are performed by the thousands. At long last hearts become so hardened to the slaughter that we feel nothing as we stand before the long piles of corpses on the road.

The Germans make us do illogical and paradoxical things. Sometimes they force us to walk, almost to run, forty miles a day without ever resting. Sometimes they make us stay at the same place in a forest for several days. Then the march goes on again, always faster and faster.

On the evening of April 6, we arrive at Buchenwald concentration camp. I believe I am one of the very few among the several thousand prisoners in our transport who still have a very small piece of bread left. I keep it safely hidden; nobody knows about it. We may at last enjoy some rest here. Completely exhausted, we all drop on the ground and lie down. When I sit down, I see my small piece of bread roll on the ground. I swiftly pick it up and put it back in my pocket. But immediately a few Jewish fellow prisoners give me their wise advice: "Listen," they say, "that Russian over there saw your bread. Don't you think that the best thing you can do now is to cut it and give us each a mouthful and get it over with before the Russian comes back and takes it from you?" As I show little enthusiasm for the idea, one of them continues, "All right, if you don't want to share it with us, at least eat it yourself, and for heaven's sake, do it before the Russian comes back."

"No, I am not going to either share it or eat it; I want to keep it for later on."

A strange feeling apparently comes over me at this moment. An inner voice must still be telling me that no one could insist on using violence to obtain something that belongs to someone else. It must be a principle deep down in the back of my mind for which I am still stubbornly fighting despite abundant evidence that I am wrong. A few minutes pass. Then seven or eight Russians, who have conferred among themselves, approach me. They have decided to attack me and take my bread. One of them shouts at me, "Adaï khleb!" ("Give me the bread!"). As I shrug to indicate that I don't have any, they all fall on me. I am thrown this way and that on the ground. They step on me until I ask for nothing more than to be allowed to breathe. Hands search my pockets. My glasses, my penknife, and an old piece of shirt that I use as a handkerchief—all that constituted my small wealth, including the bread, of course—are taken from me. The Russians release me only when they see that one of them has found my bread. Now they all throw themselves on him to get a few crumbs.

When we leave Buchenwald, the SS convoy takes us to Weimar, five miles away, where we take the train. We cover about forty-five miles by train in three days, and then we continue on foot. Later we cover another few dozen miles by train in three days, down to Dachau. From there, we proceed to the concentration camp of Dachau\* on foot. Having left Ordruf (about sixty miles above Weimar) on April 3, we finally reach Dachau on April 27.

During that tragic odyssey, from Flossenberg Concentration Camp on, and for about ten days, our transport has no food, no ration at all. Very occasionally some charitable peasants offer us a few half-raw potatoes. Many captives have become used to doing without food; they no longer have any sensation of hunger. Others, hoping to conserve their strength, eat grass. And at short intervals we hear gunshots killing those of our traveling companions who are no longer able to drag themselves along.

The column formation of hundreds of prisoners is disrupted constantly as a ceaseless stream of vehicles of all kinds carry SS and other higher personnel who are fleeing before the advance of the American troops. The SS officers in our convoy keep barking, "Aufgehen! rechte Hande!" ("Keep going! keep right!"), and strike us with their clubs. American planes fly over the convoys continually. As long as we are on foot, the American aviators, recognizing us as prisoners, leave us alone. But during our two short trips by train, we endure four air raids and suffer 150 to 200 casualties each time, not including the wounded. At night, if we are not marching, we sleep in some village barn. But most of the time, we lie down in a meadow and sleep in the mud without any blankets. Sometimes we sleep on the wet pavement of some town or city. We cross over the Danube at Straubing. And finally, on the evening of April 27, we ar-

\* Dachau concentration camp, and also the town of Dachau, in southern Germany, about twelve miles north of Munich.

rive at Dachau. The greatest disappointment awaits us there. We were hoping for a few days of rest, and signs that this camp is being prepared for evacuation plunge us into the greatest despair. The remaining prisoners in the convoy, including myself, are utterly incapable of continuing the march. If Dachau is being evacuated, we have no choice but to lie in the road and to let ourselves be killed like so many of our comrades before us. Will all the suffering of these last days—the hunger, the thirst, the rain, the blows, and wounds on our feet— have been in vain? Tomorrow or the next day, if we have to leave Dachau, almost all of us will be killed.

# 30. The Liberation

On April 29, 1945, at about five in the afternoon, strange whisperings go from mouth to mouth. The word is that the Americans are very close to Dachau and that they might arrive at any minute now. It is also being said that the SS officers have already hoisted white flags on the watchtowers. Some of us do not dare to believe such sensational good news. Although I am extremely weak, I manage to drag myself outside the Block. There, indeed, I see white flags on top of the watchtowers. But how do the prisoners come to know the glad tidings with such certainty? I don't know, but the fact is that, a few hours before the arrival of the Americans in Dachau, all of us at the camp knew that we were about to be liberated. The mortars and the machine guns gradually increase in their intensity and violence.

At about 5:30 P.M. a formidable thunder shakes the whole barrack, the entire camp. Shouts of cheer and joy from thousands of breasts reverberate all around: "They are here! The Americans! They have arrived!" "Long live the Allies! Down with the SS!" Everybody is rushing outside. Carried away with the crowd I find myself on the road—and what should I see? On the other side of the wires, the Americans are smiling and chewing gum! Some of them are on foot; others are driving their jeeps. They are waving to us. We owe them our lives. As for them, they seem to find what they have done for us a perfectly natural thing. At the same time one of my most ardent wishes during captivity becomes reality. During my two years as a prisoner, I have fervently wanted to see those SS officers, so proud and so arrogant, being taken prisoners themselves. And now the moment has come. A group of SS officers, hands in the air, are being led away by the Americans, at the point of their bayonets. All the prisoners are demanding the Germans' deaths and are calling them scoundrels, barbarians, murderers, and miserable bandits. I cry out, "God granted that I should see those SS deprived of their liberty! Now I can die in peace!"

Then the mob moves toward the big square; it is an impetuous, ungovernable torrent. On a tower at the Appellplatz, an American chaplain is trying to make himself heard.* At last there is silence. In a short prayer the chaplain gives thanks to God and praises Him for having saved us. Then we observe a minute of silence for the dead. Afterward the delirious cheering starts again. Throughout the camp there suddenly appear an amazing number of flags of the Allies: American, British, Russian, Polish, French, Greek, Belgian, Dutch, Czech, Yugoslavian, and so on. But where have all these flags come from? They must have been patiently made in secret.

On the following days, the celebration continues uninterrupted. They are gone forever, the dreary Auftehen of the morning, the torment of the evening roll call, the exhausting labor of daytime, the Kapos' savage blows, the rain, the mud, the vermin and itch, the selections, the gas chambers, the crematorium!

But alas! We the Jews have paid a high price in this war. I do not know the precise figure, but more than six

---

* The chaplain was presumably Rabbi David Eichhorn; cf. Michael Selzer, *Deliverance Day: The Last Hours at Dachau* (Philadelphia, 1978), pp. 214ff.

million Jews* are estimated to have been the victims of Nazi fury.

From those who left Greece—more than sixty thousand—fewer than two thousand survivors remain.

As for the Jews of our town, Dhidhimoteichon, and those of nearby Néa-Orestiás, from the total of 1,070 who arrived at Birkenau, about 20 have returned. Never before has such a catastrophe been recorded in the history of mankind. And the disaster has been perpetrated voluntarily, without any provocation, in a premeditated manner, coldly, methodically, by a people who only yesterday claimed to be at the forefront of civilization!

God and history alone shall be judge of this immeasurably vile and infamous crime.

Dachau-Augsburg,
June–July 1945

---

* The figure of more than six million Jews was later officially confirmed. In addition, more than six million non-Jewish civilians died in concentration camps, reprisals, bombing, and slave labor camps during the years 1939–1945.

# Postscript

The memoir ends with the liberation of Dachau. Dr. Nahon recounted some of his experiences to the editor, including the circumstances surrounding the genesis of the manuscript. These are appended here as a supplement to his testimony.

During the death march to Dachau Dr. Nahon lost contact with his friend Israel Alkabèz. The latter had collapsed a day before the column arrived at Dachau and had begged Dr. Nahon to leave him and to save himself. Then Alkabèz waited for the guard to approach and shoot him; thousands had already been shot during the horrible trek. As the guard took aim, Israel Alkabèz looked up and begged him not to shoot: "Please don't kill me, I have three daughters," he said, and the German did not shoot him. He recovered sufficiently after the column had passed and hid in the forest for a few days. Finally hunger overcame caution and he entered a village, knocked on several doors and eventually received food. When he returned after a few days, he was told by the same people: "Don't be afraid, the Americans came." He then met a column of GIs and was hailed by one driver who turned out to be a Greek American with whom he could converse in his own language. The whole contingent showered him with food and cigarettes before taking him to the hospital in Augsburg. Meanwhile Dr. Nahon, who was working in the Dachau infirmary, having arrived on the day before the liberation of the camp, remarked sadly: "It is a shame that Israel died for one day." His surprise was swallowed up in joy—still vivid after forty-five years—when he heard from his medical suppliers that his friend was to be found alive and recovering in the Augsburg hospital. They were soon reunited. While he was recovering in the hospital, Dr. Nahon finished recording the experiences of his family and coreligionists.

After his release from the hospital, Dr. Nahon was evacuated via an American train to Bari, Italy, which was then controlled by the British. There Greek Jews and Greek Christians about to be repatriated found themselves sharing barracks with some Greeks wearing German uniforms, who had in some way served with or for the Wehrmacht. Regarding these agents of their former persecutors as traitors, the Greek Christians stoned them and assaulted them physically. From Bari all the Greeks embarked by ship to Corinth, where the Jews among them were met by a delegation of Jews from Athens. All were brought by truck to Athens. Dr. Nahon returned to Dhidhimoteichon where he discovered that only perhaps twenty Jews had survived the war. He subsequently found his son and moved to Athens. In 1956 he and his son immigrated to the United States, where he practiced medicine until his retirement.

Dr. Marco Nahon, 1984

# Appendix
## The Israelite Communities of
## Dhidhimoteichon and Orestiás

<hr>

In 1979 the Central Board of Jewish Communities in Athens published a memorial volume which contains lists of names of victims from a number of Greek towns. By no means exhaustive, it is nevertheless the only epitaph for many of the Greek victims of the Holocaust. The format below follows that of the original Greek edition.

The transliteration or translation of the names follows no scholarly system. Many of the names are recognizable from their Hebrew, Greek, French, Ottoman, or Spanish origin. In most cases the Greek orthography has been preserved as an aid to the local pronunciation. Thus the spelling "Mois" reflects the use of the Greek eta or iota, while the spelling "Mous," pronounced "Mois," preserves the original upsilon. Since H is lacking in Greek (it is usually represented by an aspirate diacritical mark) the Jews generally used a Greek chi to force its pronunciation, and we have preserved this by an H in transliteration except in the case of the eta in Elias, retained to differentiate this name from the alternate Ilias, with iota. The Y in Yuda represents the Greek combination of gamma and iota. The diphthong omicron upsilon is usually rendered by U except where the sense suggests that "ou" should be retained in English. The first appearance of a name identifies its provenance. "Rasel/Rachel," for example, reflects the Greek spelling of the French pronunciation.

The lists will provide much of value and interest to researchers in various social sciences, including demography, anthropology, and sociology. Such research, which could not be undertaken here, would give us a better understanding of the generation in transition from Turkish to Greek culture as it was affected by the inherited influence of Judaeo-Spanish culture as opposed to the influx of the French and the challenge of Zionism alongside the older Hebrew religious traditions.

May their souls be bound up in the bonds of eternal life.

# Israelite Community of Dhidhimoteichon

| No. | Family Name | First Name | Father or Husband | Age |
|-----|-------------|------------|-------------------|-----|
| 1 | Aroyio | Mair | Haim | 65 |
| 2 | " | Kalo | Mair | 61 |
| 3 | " | Raphael | Mair | 19 |
| 4 | " | Samuel | Elias | 26 |
| 5 | " | Franka | Elias | 41 |
| 6 | Arenos | Luna | Nisim | 78 |
| 7 | " | Isua | Nisim | 34 |
| 8 | " | Mous/ Moise = Moses/ | Nisim | 27 |
| 9 | " | Raphael | Avraam | 39 |
| 10 | " | Nisim | Raphael | 16 |
| 11 | " | Rasel/Rachel/ | Raphael | 14 |
| 12 | " | Yoseph | Raphael | 11 |
| 13 | Adato | Yoseph | Nisim | 54 |
| 14 | " | Reina | Yoseph | 51 |
| 15 | " | Aron | Yoseph | 20 |
| 16 | " | Piza | Avraam | 64 |
| 17 | " | Ida | Avraam | 29 |
| 18 | Abulafia | Rasel | Mous | 45 |
| 19 | " | Leon | Mous | 16 |
| 20 | " | Bohor | Hiskea | 51 |
| 21 | " | Liza | Bohor | 47 |
| 22 | " | Ida | Bohor | 19 |
| 23 | " | Hiskea | Bohor | 21 |
| 24 | " | Albert | Bohor | 13 |
| 25 | Azouz | Pepo | Solomon | 54 |
| 26 | " | Doreta | Pepo | 51 |
| 27 | " | Matika | Pepo | 22 |
| 28 | " | Solomon | Pepo | 18 |
| 29 | " | Marika | Pepo | 15 |
| 30 | " | Zak | Solomon | 45 |
| 31 | " | Fortunè | Zak/Isaac/ | 36 |
| 32 | " | Solomon | Zak | 12 |
| 33 | " | Haim | Zak | 5 |

| | | | | |
|---|---|---|---|---|
| 34 | Alkalai | Albert | Siapat | 44 |
| 35 | " | Lusi | Albert | 43 |
| 36 | " | Mazalto/v/ | Siapat | 64 |
| 37 | " | Rasel | Siapat | 25 |
| 38 | " | Ruben | Siapat | 23 |
| 39 | " | Liza | Mous | 48 |
| 40 | Albalah | Siapat | Mordu | 61 |
| 41 | " | Roza | Siapat | 59 |
| 42 | " | Vitalis | Siapat | 22 |
| 43 | " | Yoseph | Siapat | 19 |
| 44 | " | Suzana | Siapat | 17 |
| 45 | Alkabes | Boulisou | Israel | 41 |
| 46 | " | Yuda | Israel | 4 |
| 47 | " | Ester | Israel | 4 |
| 48 | " | Dora | Nisim | 37 |
| 49 | " | Dezi | Nisim | 14 |
| 50 | " | Mordu | Yoseph | 60 |
| 51 | " | Sultana | Mordu | 67 |
| 52 | " | Perla | Mordu | 27 |
| 53 | " | Aaron | Mordu | 24 |
| 54 | " | Yako/b/ | Isaak | 40 |
| 55 | " | Perla | Yako | 43 |
| 56 | " | Sultana | Yako | 10 |
| 57 | " | Isaak | Yako | 7 |
| 58 | " | Sara | Yako | 3 |
| 59 | " | Aron | Kemal | 66 |
| 60 | " | Bulka | Aron | 61 |
| 61 | " | Samuel | Aron | 29 |
| 62 | " | Luna | Aron | 30 |
| 63 | " | Zubul | Aron | 18 |
| 64 | " | Avraam | Samuel | 68 |
| 65 | " | Viktoria | Avraam | 36 |
| 66 | " | Elias | Avraam | 22 |
| 67 | " | Ines | Avraam | 21 |
| 68 | " | Estrea | Mordohai | 66 |
| 69 | " | Raphael | Avraam | 45 |
| 70 | " | Zubul | Raphael | 44 |
| 71 | " | Avraam | Raphael | 13 |
| 72 | " | Aaron | Raphael | 5 |
| 73 | " | Siapat | Yuda | 64 |

| 74 | Alkabes | Dudu | Siapat | 65 |
|---|---|---|---|---|
| 75 | " | Elias | Tsilibi | 78 |
| 76 | " | Buka | Elias | 66 |
| 77 | " | Rasel | Elias | 24 |
| 78 | " | Reva | Elias | 21 |
| 79 | " | Aron | Yuda | 63 |
| 80 | " | Rasel | Aron | 46 |
| 81 | " | Leon | Aron | 18 |
| 82 | " | Haim | Avraam | 61 |
| 83 | " | Dina | Haim | 58 |
| 84 | " | Ester | Haim | 21 |
| 85 | " | Yantov | Haim | 17 |
| 86 | " | Menase | Haim | 15 |
| 87 | " | Yoseph | Isaak | 54 |
| 88 | " | Klara | Yoseph | 46 |
| 89 | " | Isaak | Yoseph | 23 |
| 90 | " | Mordu | Yoseph | 23 |
| 91 | " | Sultana | Yoseph | 16 |
| 92 | " | Roza | Yoseph | 13 |
| 93 | " | Yoseph | Samuel | 65 |
| 94 | " | Rena | Yoseph | 57 |
| 95 | " | Ziak/Isaak/ | Yoseph | 30 |
| 96 | " | Dona | Yoseph | 24 |
| 97 | " | Mathildi | Yoseph | 20 |
| 98 | " | Prezenti | Yoseph | 17 |
| 99 | " | Yoseph | Yuda | 62 |
| 100 | " | Perla | Yoseph | 56 |
| 101 | " | Roza | Nisim | 24 |
| 102 | " | Neama | Yoseph | 11 |
| 103 | " | Bohor | Avraam | 64 |
| 104 | " | Sara | Bohor | 63 |
| 105 | " | Rasel | Bohor | 30 |
| 106 | " | Tselebi | Elias | 39 |
| 107 | " | Sultana | Tselebi | 36 |
| 108 | " | Rasel | Tselebi | 11 |
| 109 | " | Mazalto | Yako | 69 |
| 110 | " | Zubul | Avraam | 35 |
| 111 | " | Haim | Siapat | 49 |
| 112 | " | Revekka | Haim | 37 |

| 113 | Alkabes | Menase | Haim | 12 |
|---|---|---|---|---|
| 114 | " | Rasel | Haim | 6 |
| 115 | " | Albert | Bohor | 39 |
| 116 | " | Simha | Albert | 35 |
| 117 | " | Ester | Albert | 17 |
| 118 | " | Mous | Avraam | 11 |
| 119 | " | Tselebi | Isaak | 52 |
| 120 | " | Ida | Tselebi | 51 |
| 121 | " | Retzina | Tselebi | 21 |
| 122 | " | Mous | Yako | 53 |
| 123 | " | Sara | Mous | 46 |
| 124 | " | Sol | Mous | 23 |
| 125 | " | Yako | Mous | 17 |
| 126 | " | Avraam | Mous | 11 |
| 127 | " | Siapat | Bohor | 34 |
| 128 | " | Mathildi | Siapat | 30 |
| 129 | " | Sara | Siapat | 4 |
| 130 | " | Mous | Siapat | 2 |
| 131 | " | Luna | Ouziel | 30 |
| 132 | " | Raphael | Ouziel | 6 |
| 133 | " | Ines | Ouziel | 9 |
| 134 | " | Kemal | Sapat | 38 |
| 135 | " | Ida | Kemal | 30 |
| 136 | " | Vitali | Kemal | 8 |
| 137 | " | Mathildi | Kemal | 4 |
| 138 | " | Solomon | Elias | 31 |
| 139 | " | Liza | Solomon | 30 |
| 140 | " | Elias | Solomon | 5 |
| 141 | " | Rasel | Solomon | 2 |
| 142 | " | Kemal | Avraam | 37 |
| 143 | " | Sultana | Kemal | 26 |
| 144 | " | Zubul | Kemal | 1 |
| 145 | Aroyio | Vitali | Mair | 34 |
| 146 | " | Retzina | Vitali | 32 |
| 147 | " | Kalo | Vitali | 8 |
| 148 | " | Mair | Vitali | 5 |
| 149 | " | Dona | Vitali | 1 |
| 150 | Alkalai | Yantof/ Yomtov/ | Siapat | 38 |

| 151 | Alkalai | Sofi | Yantof | 33 |
|---|---|---|---|---|
| 152 | " | Mathildi | Yantof | 6 |
| 153 | Aroyio | Rakel | Iakov | 29 |
| 154 | " | Kalo | Iakov | 4 |
| 155 | Atias | Dudu | Isaak | 52 |
| 156 | " | Sara | Isaak | 19 |
| 157 | " | Zubul | Isaak | 17 |
| 158 | Benaroyia | Avraam | David | 61 |
| 159 | " | Dudo | Avraam | 55 |
| 160 | " | David | Avraam | 28 |
| 161 | " | Iosef | Avraam | 23 |
| 162 | " | Bohora | Avraam | 85 |
| 163 | Doenias | Mous | Isaak | 64 |
| 164 | " | Fortunè | Mous | 55 |
| 165 | " | Isaak | Menase | 81 |
| 166 | " | Benvenida | Isaak | 59 |
| 167 | " | Aron | Isaak | 40 |
| 168 | " | Menase | Isaak | 38 |
| 169 | " | Franka | Isaak | 24 |
| 170 | " | Sultana | Isaak | 20 |
| 171 | " | Isaak | Haim | 46 |
| 172 | " | Nisim | Haim | 34 |
| 173 | " | Liza | Haim | 31 |
| 174 | " | Zubul | Isaak | 87 |
| 175 | " | Iakov | Menase | 59 |
| 176 | " | Sultana | Iakov | 54 |
| 177 | " | Ester | Iakov | 32 |
| 178 | " | Bela | Iakov | 28 |
| 179 | " | Liza | Iakov | 25 |
| 180 | " | Ines | Iakov | 20 |
| 181 | " | Roza | Iakov | 15 |
| 182 | " | Yako | Isaak | 79 |
| 183 | " | Roza | Yako | 73 |
| 184 | " | Menase | Yako | 45 |
| 185 | " | Aaron | Iakov | 33 |
| 186 | " | Ester | Aaron | 32 |
| 187 | " | Iakov | Aaron | 6 |
| 188 | Dekalo | Ester | David | 77 |
| 189 | " | Leon | David | 36 |

| 190 | Dekalo | Markos | Yudea | 51 |
|------|--------|--------|-------|-----|
| 191 | " | Perla | Markos | 45 |
| 192 | " | Rahel | Markos | 22 |
| 193 | " | Luna | Markos | 20 |
| 194 | " | Isaak | David | 53 |
| 195 | " | Mathildi | Isaak | 41 |
| 196 | " | Ēster | Isaak | 22 |
| 197 | " | Zali | Isaak | 22 |
| 198 | " | Sultana | Isaak | 11 |
| 199 | " | Bohora | Kemal | 66 |
| 200 | " | Iakov | Kemal | 25 |
| 201 | " | Nisim | Kemal | 23 |
| 202 | " | Pepo | David | 34 |
| 203 | " | Neama | Pepo | 32 |
| 204 | " | Ester | Pepo | 9 |
| 205 | " | David | Pepo | 6 |
| 206 | " | Isaak | Kemal | 29 |
| 207 | " | Zelda | Isaak | 26 |
| 208 | " | Raphael | Kemal | 35 |
| 209 | " | Estrea | Raphael | 35 |
| 210 | " | Virzini | Raphael | 8 |
| 211 | " | Samuel | Raphael | 4 |
| 212 | Jivré | Fortunè | Tselebi | 70 |
| 213 | " | Nisim | Tselebi | 42 |
| 214 | " | Viktoria | Nisim | 33 |
| 215 | " | Eliezer | Nisim | 8 |
| 216 | " | Samuel | Nisim | 3 |
| 217 | " | Rasel | David | 71 |
| 218 | " | Albert | David | 41 |
| 219 | " | Marika | Albert | 32 |
| 220 | " | David | Albert | 7 |
| 221 | " | Mair | David | 53 |
| 222 | " | Fortunè | Mair | 47 |
| 223 | " | Roza | Mair | 16 |
| 224 | " | Rasel | Mair | 10 |
| 225 | " | Mous | Haim | 32 |
| 226 | " | Bidu | Raphael | 61 |
| 227 | " | Isaak | Raphael | 38 |
| 228 | " | Neama | Raphael | 30 |

| 229 | Jivré | Zubul | Raphael | 27 |
| 230 | " | Ines | Raphael | 34 |
| 231 | " | Solomon | Iakov | 78 |
| 232 | " | Roza | Isaak | 30 |
| 233 | " | Raphael | Isaak | 8 |
| 234 | " | Viktoria | Isaak | 3 |
| 235 | " | Isaak | Solomon | 40 |
| 236 | " | Viktoria | Isaak | 34 |
| 237 | " | Rika | Solomon | 81 |
| 238 | " | Solomon | Isaak | 10 |
| 239 | " | Mous | Isaak | 7 |
| 240 | " | Dina | Isua | 54 |
| 241 | " | Virzini | Isua | 33 |
| 242 | " | Mous | Isua | 27 |
| 243 | " | Solomon | Bohor | 53 |
| 244 | " | Retzina | Solomon | 40 |
| 245 | " | Ester | Solomon | 16 |
| 246 | " | Berta | Solomon | 7 |
| 247 | " | Fortunè | Solomon | 5 |
| 248 | " | Aaron | David | 59 |
| 249 | " | Zubul | Aaron | 47 |
| 250 | " | David | Aaron | 22 |
| 251 | " | Retzina | Aaron | 18 |
| 252 | " | Yako | Aaron | 15 |
| 253 | " | Nisim | Bohor | 56 |
| 254 | " | Viktoria | Nisim | 47 |
| 255 | " | Ester | Nisim | 20 |
| 256 | " | Haim | Nisim | 18 |
| 257 | " | Rika | Vitali | 37 |
| 258 | " | David | Vitali | 17 |
| 259 | " | Yako | Vitali | 15 |
| 260 | " | Samuel | Vitali | 14 |
| 261 | " | Ester | David | 39 |
| 262 | " | David | Eliezer | 35 |
| 263 | " | Kler | Albert | 35 |
| 264 | " | Albert | Eliezer | 46 |
| 265 | " | Eliezer | Albert | 12 |
| 266 | " | Vitali | Solomon | 37 |
| 267 | " | Retzina | Vitale | 41 |

| 268 | Jivrè | Ester | Vitale | 13 |
|---|---|---|---|---|
| 269 | " | Mair | Vitale | 9 |
| 270 | " | Revekka | Vitale | 4 |
| 271 | " | Mous | Isaak | 59 |
| 272 | " | Ester | Mous | 54 |
| 273 | " | Yoseph | Mous | 28 |
| 274 | " | Ameli | Mous | 27 |
| 275 | " | Suzana | Mous | 27 |
| 276 | " | Venuta | Mous | 20 |
| 277 | " | Marko | Mair | 50 |
| 278 | " | Vidu | Marko | 39 |
| 279 | " | Neama | Marko | 19 |
| 280 | " | Mair | Marko | 15 |
| 281 | " | Revekka | Marko | 13 |
| 282 | " | Haim | Iakov | 72 |
| 283 | " | Rasel | Haim | 62 |
| 284 | " | Luna | Haim | 30 |
| 285 | " | Nisim | Haim | 23 |
| 286 | " | Ruben | Haim | 22 |
| 287 | " | Yoseph | Siapat | 46 |
| 288 | " | Ester | Siapat | 31 |
| 289 | " | Mazalto | Siapat | 12 |
| 290 | " | Eliezer | Solomon | 50 |
| 291 | " | Roza | Eliezer | 44 |
| 292 | " | Solomon | Eliezer | 22 |
| 293 | " | Haim | Eliezer | 19 |
| 294 | " | Israel | Eliezer | 13 |
| 295 | " | Isaak | Eliezer | 8 |
| 296 | " | Avraam | Nisim | 65 |
| 297 | " | Revekka | Avraam | 54 |
| 298 | " | Israel | Avraam | 20 |
| 299 | " | Fortunè | Israel | 61 |
| 300 | " | Solomon | Israel | 24 |
| 301 | " | Revekka | Siapat | 34 |
| 302 | " | Sol | Yuda | 36 |
| 303 | " | Berta | Yuda | 34 |
| 304 | " | Fortunè | Mair | 64 |
| 305 | " | Leon | Mair | 30 |
| 306 | " | Rasel | Mair | 24 |

| 307 | Jivré | David | Mair | 22 |
|---|---|---|---|---|
| 308 | " | Nisim | Isua | 57 |
| 309 | " | Fortunè | Nisim | 52 |
| 310 | " | Ester | Nisim | 29 |
| 311 | " | Yoseph | Nisim | 17 |
| 312 | " | Roza | Nisim | 13 |
| 313 | " | Dona | Isua | 67 |
| 314 | " | David | Isua | 65 |
| 315 | " | Roza | David | 56 |
| 316 | " | Isaak | Siakaton | 40 |
| 317 | " | Neama | Isaak | 38 |
| 318 | " | Solomon | Mair | 45 |
| 319 | " | Revekka | Siakaton | 31 |
| 320 | " | Bohor | Haim | 39 |
| 321 | " | Siniora | Bohor | 34 |
| 322 | " | Haim | Bohor | 8 |
| 323 | " | Ines | Bohor | 2 |
| 324 | " | Kemal | Haim | 33 |
| 325 | " | Tzoya | Kemal | 29 |
| 326 | " | Haim | Kemal | 1 |
| 327 | " | Yoseph | Haim | 44 |
| 328 | " | Boulisou | Yoseph | 32 |
| 329 | " | Ester | Yoseph | 9 |
| 330 | " | Mathildi | Yoseph | 6 |
| 331 | " | Pepo | Raphael | 35 |
| 332 | " | Ester | Pepo | 29 |
| 333 | " | Raphael | Pepo | 4 |
| 334 | Ergas | Reina | Haim | 68 |
| 335 | " | Isaak | Haim | 39 |
| 336 | " | Revekka | Isaak | 31 |
| 337 | " | Retzina | Isaak | 10 |
| 338 | " | Haim | Isaak | 4 |
| 339 | Eskenazy | Fortunè | Beniamin | 35 |
| 340 | " | Sara | Solomon | 59 |
| 341 | " | Vitali | Solomon | 38 |
| 342 | " | Klara | Solomon | 33 |
| 343 | " | Roza | Solomon | 30 |
| 344 | " | Marko | Solomon | 27 |
| 345 | " | Sultana | Solomon | 24 |

| 346 | Eskenazy | Yantov | Haim | 59 |
|---|---|---|---|---|
| 347 | " | Liza | Yantov | 53 |
| 348 | " | Ester | Yantov | 23 |
| 349 | " | Ida | Mous | 30 |
| 350 | " | Retzina | Isaak | 32 |
| 351 | " | Mous | Isaak | 6 |
| 352 | " | Simon | Yakov | 65 |
| 353 | " | Roza | Simon | 51 |
| 354 | " | Zubul | Simon | 21 |
| 355 | " | Zak | Simon | 17 |
| 356 | " | Albert | Haim | 52 |
| 357 | " | Rasel | Albert | 47 |
| 358 | " | Haim | Albert | 20 |
| 359 | " | Ester | Albert | 17 |
| 360 | " | Marko | Eliezer | 45 |
| 361 | " | Revekka | Marko | 44 |
| 362 | " | Eliezer | Marko | 15 |
| 363 | " | Sultana | Marko | 11 |
| 364 | " | Haim | Marko | 5 |
| 365 | " | David | Solomon | 56 |
| 366 | " | Leon | Eliezer | 29 |
| 367 | " | Ester | Bohor | 71 |
| 368 | " | Mair | Bohor | 41 |
| 369 | " | Marko | Bohor | 34 |
| 370 | Zamero | Zak | Mous | 54 |
| 371 | " | Luna | Zak | 48 |
| 372 | " | Sultana | Zak | 26 |
| 373 | " | Salvator | Zak | 23 |
| 374 | " | Viktoria | Zak | 20 |
| 375 | " | Mathildi | Zak | 17 |
| 376 | Kasuto | Roza | Bohor | 67 |
| 377 | " | Eliezer | Bohor | 36 |
| 378 | " | Fortunè | Eliezer | 33 |
| 379 | " | Roza | Eliezer | 11 |
| 380 | " | Aron | Eliezer | 9 |
| 381 | " | Samuel | Isua | 44 |
| 382 | " | Israel | Isua | 28 |
| 383 | " | Revekka | Samuel | 15 |
| 384 | " | Solomon | Samuel | 10 |

| | | | |
|---|---|---|---|
| 385 | Kasuto | Bea | Samuel | 8 |
| 386 | " | Ines | Isaak | 24 |
| 387 | " | Avraam | Isua | 6 |
| 388 | " | Mousis | Isua | 21 |
| 389 | " | Nisim | Bohor | 33 |
| 390 | " | Iakov | Nisim | 6 |
| 391 | " | Neama | Nisim | 28 |
| 392 | Kaneti | Avraam | Isaak | 59 |
| 393 | " | Estrea | Avraam | 53 |
| 394 | " | Roza | Avraam | 17 |
| 395 | " | Pulina | Avraam | 15 |
| 396 | " | Fanè | Avraam | 13 |
| 397 | " | Bohor | David | 83 |
| 398 | " | Yuda | Bohor | 60 |
| 399 | " | Roza | Yuda | 51 |
| 400 | " | Ines | Yuda | 25 |
| 401 | " | Roza | Bohor | 41 |
| 402 | " | David | Isaak | 52 |
| 403 | " | Virzini/ | David | 43 |
| | | Virginia/ | | |
| 404 | " | Pulina | David | 21 |
| 405 | " | Isaak | David | 19 |
| 406 | " | Bulisu | David | 14 |
| 407 | " | Isaak | David | 82 |
| 408 | " | Pava | Isaak | 86 |
| 409 | " | Nisim | Siapat | 31 |
| 410 | " | Sultana | Isaak | 71 |
| 411 | " | David | Bohor | 68 |
| 412 | " | Liza | David | 59 |
| 413 | " | Bohora | Nisim | 67 |
| 414 | " | Simon | Avraam | 70 |
| 415 | " | Bienvenira | Simon | 66 |
| 416 | " | Avraam | Nisim | 38 |
| 417 | " | Sohoula | Avraam | 37 |
| 418 | " | Nisim | Avraam | 15 |
| 419 | " | Liza | Avraam | 14 |
| 420 | " | Yoseph | Avraam | 8 |
| 421 | " | Markos | Avraam | 4 |
| 422 | " | Isua | Siapat | 40 |

| 423 | Kaneti | Revekka | Isua | 35 |
|-----|--------|---------|------|-----|
| 424 | " | Sarra | Isua | 1 |
| 425 | " | Yako | Nisim | 28 |
| 426 | " | Perla | Yako | 28 |
| 427 | " | Luna | Yako | 4 |
| 428 | " | Vitali | Siapat | 34 |
| 429 | " | Mazalto | Vitali | 27 |
| 430 | Kamhi | Yoseph | Siapat | 35 |
| 431 | " | Zubul | Yoseph | 30 |
| 432 | " | Perla | Yoseph | 10 |
| 433 | " | Sarika | Yoseph | 6 |
| 434 | Kazes | Solomon | Yoseph | 72 |
| 435 | " | Tzamila | Solomon | 71 |
| 436 | Litsi | Mous | Solomon | 52 |
| 437 | " | Perla | Mous | 49 |
| 438 | " | Sultana | Mous | 21 |
| 439 | " | Yako | Mous | 19 |
| 440 | " | Haim | Mous | 13 |
| 441 | " | Sohoula | Menahem | 61 |
| 442 | " | Ines | Menahem | 26 |
| 443 | " | Sultana | Menahem | 23 |
| 444 | " | Israel | Hiskea | 34 |
| 445 | " | Hanoum | Hiskea | 71 |
| 446 | " | Roza | Israel | 35 |
| 447 | " | Hana | Israel | 9 |
| 448 | " | Sultana | Israel | 6 |
| 449 | " | Sarra | Nisim | 66 |
| 450 | " | Mous | Avraam | 64 |
| 451 | " | Ester | Mous | 53 |
| 452 | " | Nisim | Mous | 24 |
| 453 | " | Perla | Mous | 21 |
| 454 | " | Kalo | Mous | 18 |
| 455 | " | Aaron | Mous | 16 |
| 456 | " | Markos | Solomon | 44 |
| 457 | " | Zubul | Markos | 38 |
| 458 | " | Bohor | Solomon | 57 |
| 459 | " | Dudu | Bohor | 54 |
| 460 | " | Nisim | Bohor | 24 |
| 461 | " | Solomon | Bohor | 21 |

| 462 | Litsi | Menahem | Bohor | 4 |
|-----|-------|---------|-------|-----|
| 463 | " | Nisim | Hiskea | 43 |
| 464 | " | Fortunè | Nisim | 43 |
| 465 | " | Sara | Nisim | 17 |
| 466 | " | Estrea | Nisim | 14 |
| 467 | " | Mari | Nisim | 11 |
| 468 | " | Mair | Nisim | 8 |
| 469 | " | Yuda | Solomon | 51 |
| 470 | " | Luna | Yuda | 43 |
| 471 | " | Liza | Yuda | 20 |
| 472 | " | Berta | Yuda | 19 |
| 473 | " | Solomon | Yuda | 12 |
| 474 | " | Israel | Solomon | 52 |
| 475 | " | Rasel | Israel | 49 |
| 476 | " | Estrea | Israel | 21 |
| 477 | " | Nisim | Israel | 19 |
| 478 | " | Aron | Israel | 16 |
| 479 | " | Mous | Aaron | 46 |
| 480 | " | Albert | Mous | 18 |
| 481 | " | Sultana | Mous | 10 |
| 482 | " | Isupha | Bohor | 50 |
| 483 | " | Revekka | Isupha | 46 |
| 484 | " | Zubul | Isupha | 18 |
| 485 | " | Aron | Isupha | 16 |
| 486 | " | Zak | Isupha | 13 |
| 487 | " | Zubul | Bohor | 76 |
| 488 | " | Yoseph | Isupha | 11 |
| 489 | " | Solomon | Isupha | 8 |
| 490 | " | Ester | Isupha | 6 |
| 491 | " | Bulka | David | 71 |
| 492 | " | Maria | David | 33 |
| 493 | " | Siapat | David | 29 |
| 494 | " | Yako | David | 28 |
| 495 | " | Albert | David | 37 |
| 496 | " | Rasel | Albert | 36 |
| 497 | " | Sultana | Albert | 14 |
| 498 | " | David | Albert | 11 |
| 499 | " | Berta | Albert | 7 |
| 500 | " | Isaak | Aaron | 36 |

| 501 | Litsi | Aron | Isaak | 12 |
|---|---|---|---|---|
| 502 | " | Hanum | Aron | 71 |
| 503 | " | Yako | Aron | 9 |
| 504 | " | Revekka | Isaak | 8 |
| 505 | " | Nina | Isaak | 32 |
| 506 | " | Isaak | Mousion | 31 |
| 507 | " | Rasel | Isaak | 31 |
| 508 | " | Ester | Isaak | 9 |
| 509 | " | Liza | Isaak | 4 |
| 510 | " | Samuel | Menahem | 30 |
| 511 | " | Ester | Samuel | 23 |
| 512 | " | Simha | Samuel | 4 |
| 513 | " | Nisim | David | 30 |
| 514 | " | Sultana | Nisim | 29 |
| 515 | " | David | Nisim | 1 |
| 516 | Levi | Nisim | Sabetai | 35 |
| 517 | " | Roza | Nisim | 34 |
| 518 | " | Liza | Nisim | 11 |
| 519 | " | Berta | Nisim | 9 |
| 520 | " | Sabetai | Nisim | 5 |
| 521 | " | Sultana | Nisim | 2 |
| 522 | Makriso | Mous | Avraam | 64 |
| 523 | " | Sinora | Mous | 58 |
| 524 | Bahar | Raphael | Yuda | 86 |
| 525 | " | Mari | Raphael | 56 |
| 526 | " | Markos | Raphael | 36 |
| 527 | " | Ester | Yoseph | 69 |
| 528 | " | Aron | Yoseph | 23 |
| 529 | " | Bulisu | Avraam | 76 |
| 530 | " | Leon | Solomon | 59 |
| 531 | " | Sultana | Leon | 46 |
| 532 | " | Solomon | Leon | 29 |
| 533 | " | Revekka | Leon | 24 |
| 534 | " | Mari | Leon | 8 |
| 535 | " | Nisim | Solomon | 39 |
| 536 | " | Ester | Nisim | 39 |
| 537 | " | Zelda | Nisim | 11 |
| 538 | " | Roza | Nisim | 10 |
| 539 | " | Revekka | Nisim | 6 |

| | | | | |
|---|---|---|---|---|
| 540 | Bahar | Tzoya | Nisim | 2 |
| 541 | " | Yantov | Haim | 73 |
| 542 | " | Ester | Yantov | 61 |
| 543 | " | Ines | Yantov | 30 |
| 544 | " | Oro | Yantov | 22 |
| 545 | " | Roza | Yuda | 63 |
| 546 | " | Sultana | Yuda | 25 |
| 547 | " | Roza | Mous | 39 |
| 548 | " | Vitali | Mous | 16 |
| 549 | " | Ines | Mous | 14 |
| 550 | " | Zelda | Mous | 12 |
| 551 | " | Yako | Isaak | 50 |
| 552 | " | Intra | Yako | 50 |
| 553 | " | Sultana | Avraam | 57 |
| 554 | " | Karolini | Avraam | 30 |
| 555 | " | Natan | Nisim | 68 |
| 556 | " | Franka | Notan | 53 |
| 557 | " | Rahel | Notan | 22 |
| 558 | " | Isaak | Yuda | 66 |
| 559 | " | Revekka | Isaak | 35 |
| 560 | " | Leon | Isaak | 32 |
| 561 | " | Yako | Isaak | 30 |
| 562 | " | Nisim | Isaak | 25 |
| 563 | " | Avraam | Nisim | 63 |
| 564 | " | Klara | Avraam | 70 |
| 565 | " | Nisim | Avraam | 38 |
| 566 | " | Markos | Avraam | 31 |
| 567 | " | Haim | Sento | 66 |
| 568 | " | Luna | Haim | 56 |
| 569 | " | Antzel | Haim | 30 |
| 570 | " | Bea | Haim | 23 |
| 571 | " | Rena | Haim | 21 |
| 572 | " | Nisim | Haim | 17 |
| 573 | " | Nisim | Isaak | 46 |
| 574 | " | Verzini | Nisim | 44 |
| 575 | " | Isaak | Nisim | 18 |
| 576 | " | Yoseph | Nisim | 16 |
| 577 | " | Mathildi | Nisim | 13 |
| 578 | " | Nisim | David | 41 |

| | | | |
|---|---|---|---|
| 579 | Bahar | Zubul | Nisim | 29 |
| 580 | " | Estrea | Nisim | 4 |
| 581 | " | David | Nisim | 2 |
| 582 | " | Yuda | Yoseph | 33 |
| 583 | " | Ester | Yuda | 32 |
| 584 | " | Ioseph | Yuda | 1 |
| 585 | Molho | Roza | Samuel | 58 |
| 586 | " | Israel | Samuel | 33 |
| 587 | " | Rasel | Samuel | 28 |
| 588 | " | Mous | Samuel | 23 |
| 589 | " | Isaak | Samuel | 38 |
| 590 | " | Fortunè | Isaak | 33 |
| 591 | " | Samuel | Isaak | 9 |
| 592 | " | Haim | Isaak | 6 |
| 593 | " | Roza | Isaak | 3 |
| 594 | Medina | Sara | Isaak | 62 |
| 595 | " | Mariam | Musion | 63 |
| 596 | Matziar | Nisim | Avraam | 62 |
| 597 | " | Luna | Nisim | 48 |
| 598 | " | Albert | Nisim | 25 |
| 599 | " | Perla | Nisim | 20 |
| 600 | Misdrahi | Isaak | Solomon | 43 |
| 601 | " | Roza | Isaak | 32 |
| 602 | " | Liza | Isaak | 11 |
| 603 | " | Sultana | Isaak | 7 |
| 604 | Menase | Rasel | Isaak | 59 |
| 605 | " | Raphael | Isaak | 28 |
| 606 | " | Solomon | Isaak | 22 |
| 607 | Modiano | Solomon | Avraam | 78 |
| 608 | " | Bidu | Solomon | 63 |
| 609 | " | Avraam | Solomon | 38 |
| 610 | " | Sinorou | Solomon | 40 |
| 611 | " | Mazalto | Solomon | 37 |
| 612 | Nahon | Simha | Mous | 63 |
| 613 | " | Inta | Mous | 29 |
| 614 | " | Ziak | Mous | 29 |
| 615 | " | Aaron | Mous | 23 |
| 616 | " | Menase | Aron | 39 |
| 617 | " | Revekka | Menase | 35 |

| 618 | Nahon | Aron | Menase | 12 |
|---|---|---|---|---|
| 619 | " | Inta | Menase | 8 |
| 620 | " | Sara | Marko | 40 |
| 621 | " | Estela | Marko | 13 |
| 622 | " | Haim | Mordehai | 77 |
| 623 | " | Bulisu | Haim | 74 |
| 624 | " | Rasel | Haim | 28 |
| 625 | " | Menase | Haim | 37 |
| 626 | " | Roza | Menase | 40 |
| 627 | " | Haim | Menase | 10 |
| 628 | " | Berta | Menase | 2 |
| 629 | Naoum | Samuel | Mous | 34 |
| 630 | " | Retzina | Samuel | 33 |
| 631 | Nahmias | Mous | Eliezer | 64 |
| 632 | " | Virzini | Mous | 51 |
| 633 | " | Samuel | Mous | 26 |
| 634 | " | Lina | Mous | 20 |
| 635 | " | Elias | Eliezer | 62 |
| 636 | " | Luna | Elias | 48 |
| 637 | " | Virginia | Prezenti | 34 |
| 638 | " | Bela | Prezenti | 32 |
| 639 | " | Elias | Prezenti | 29 |
| 640 | " | Mous | Bohor | 46 |
| 641 | " | Berta | Mous | 36 |
| 642 | " | Virginia | Mous | 14 |
| 643 | " | Elias | Mous | 6 |
| 644 | " | Kalo | Bohor | 61 |
| 645 | " | Rasel | Bohor | 29 |
| 646 | " | Solomon | Mous | 29 |
| 647 | " | Rasel | Solomon | 28 |
| 648 | " | Ester | Solomon | 1 |
| 649 | Pinhas | Avraam | Yoseph | 22 |
| 650 | " | Simha | Avraam | 23 |
| 651 | " | Mordu | Sason | 51 |
| 652 | " | Dudu | Mordu | 46 |
| 653 | " | Makona | Mordu | 23 |
| 654 | " | Phanè | Mordu | 20 |
| 655 | " | Nisim | Mordu | 15 |
| 656 | " | Leon | Mordu | 12 |

| 657 | Pinhas | Yoseph | Samuel | 62 |
|------|--------|--------|--------|-----|
| 658 | " | Samuel | Yoseph | 32 |
| 659 | " | Maria | Yoseph | 23 |
| 660 | " | Haim | Yoseph | 15 |
| 661 | " | Kalo | Samuel | 23 |
| 662 | " | Yoseph | Samuel | 3 |
| 663 | Peres | Haim | Elias | 44 |
| 664 | " | Rasel | Haim | 43 |
| 665 | " | Elias | Haim | 19 |
| 666 | " | Leon-Yuda | Haim | 16 |
| 667 | " | Bolisu | Haim | 15 |
| 668 | " | Ester | Haim | 12 |
| 669 | " | David | Haim | 7 |
| 670 | " | Iakov | Haim | 4 |
| 671 | Sini | Mordu | Yantov | 53 |
| 672 | " | Sara | Mordu | 49 |
| 673 | " | Aaron | Mordu | 18 |
| 674 | " | Yantov | Mordu | 13 |
| 675 | " | Isaak | Aaron | 59 |
| 676 | " | Sultana | Isaak | 45 |
| 677 | " | Ida | Isaak | 23 |
| 678 | " | Aaron | Isaak | 21 |
| 679 | " | Zulet | Isaak | 18 |
| 680 | " | Samuel | Isaak | 8 |
| 681 | " | Yuda | Yanto | 54 |
| 682 | " | Revekka | Yanto | 41 |
| 683 | " | Liza | Yanto | 18 |
| 684 | " | Sara | Yanto | 14 |
| 685 | " | Tzamilia | Yanto | 6 |
| 686 | " | Mathildi | Yanto | 4 |
| 687 | " | Mous | Yanto | 58 |
| 688 | " | Ester | Mous | 49 |
| 689 | " | Bidu | Mous | 20 |
| 690 | " | Liza | Mous | 18 |
| 691 | " | Roza | Mous | 14 |
| 692 | Saduk | Ziak | Samuel | 48 |
| 693 | " | Dudu | Ziak | 44 |
| 694 | " | Luna | Ziak | 17 |
| 695 | " | Zubul | Ziak | 15 |

| 696 | Saduk | Bea | Ziak | 14 |
|------|-------|-----|------|-----|
| 697 | " | Roza | Ziak | 10 |
| 698 | " | Samuel | Ziak | 6 |
| 699 | Sarphati | Mous | Aaron | 63 |
| 700 | " | Bolisu | Mous | 61 |
| 701 | " | Solomon | Mous | 20 |
| 702 | Tarabolus | David | Nisim | 55 |
| 703 | " | Klara | David | 56 |
| 704 | " | Mathildi | David | 15 |
| 705 | " | Roza | David | 14 |
| 706 | " | Aaron | Nisim | 69 |
| 707 | " | Luna | Aaron | 63 |
| 708 | " | Yoseph | Aaron | 21 |
| 709 | " | Rasel | Mous | 64 |
| 710 | " | Yuda | Mous | 34 |
| 711 | " | Sultana | Mous | 22 |
| 712 | " | Bohor | Samuel | 76 |
| 713 | " | Estrea | Bohor | 71 |
| 714 | " | Adela | Nisim | 37 |
| 715 | " | Nisim | Mous | 37 |
| 716 | " | Roza | Nisim | 33 |
| 717 | " | Ester | Nisim | 4 |
| 718 | " | Nisim | Aaron | 25 |
| 719 | " | Ester | Nisim | 23 |
| 720 | Phints/Fitz? | Haim | Yuda | 49 |
| 721 | " | Rena | Haim | 37 |
| 722 | " | Ester | Haim | 17 |
| 723 | " | Siniora | Haim | 15 |
| 724 | " | Kolomba | Haim | 11 |
| 725 | " | Yuda | Haim | 9 |
| 726 | " | Siapat | Yuda | 38 |
| 727 | " | Sultana | Siapat | 36 |
| 728 | " | Palomba | Siapat | 16 |
| 729 | " | Zalika | Siapat | 13 |
| 730 | " | Ester | Siapat | 10 |
| 731 | " | Nisim | Siapat | 6 |

# Israelite Community of Orestiás

| No. | Family Name | First Name | Father or Husband | Age |
|-----|-------------|------------|-------------------|-----|
| 1 | Eskenazi | Tselebi | Mordohai | 64 |
| 2 | " | Ines | Tselebi | 29 |
| 3 | " | Kolomba | Tselebi | 21 |
| 4 | Kalbo | Israel | Solomon | 57 |
| 5 | " | Rika | Israel | 45 |
| 6 | " | Isaak | Israel | 20 |
| 7 | " | Fortunè | Israel | 16 |
| 8 | " | Albert | Israel | 8 |
| 9 | " | Mordu | Solomon | 54 |
| 10 | " | Matilda | Mordu | 49 |
| 11 | " | Viktoria | Mordu | 20 |
| 12 | " | Sabetai | Mordu | 16 |
| 13 | " | Mois | Solomon | 43 |
| 14 | " | Klara | Mois | 37 |
| 15 | " | Solomon | Mois | 11 |
| 16 | " | Mair | Mois | 9 |
| 17 | " | Yuda | Solomon | 36 |
| 18 | " | Rika | Yuda | 31 |
| 19 | " | Viktoria | Yuda | 12 |
| 20 | " | Roza | Yuda | 8 |
| 21 | Binun | Mois | Solomon | 49 |
| 22 | " | Bolissu | Mois | 42 |
| 23 | " | Sophia | Mois | 17 |
| 24 | " | Solomon | Mois | 13 |
| 25 | " | Israel | Mois | 8 |
| 26 | Muaraph | Rouphat | Solomon | 30 |
| 27 | " | Roza | Rouphat | 43 |
| 28 | " | Solomon | Rouphat | 17 |
| 29 | " | Rika | Rouphat | 14 |
| 30 | " | Avraam | Rouphat | 8 |
| 31 | " | Bohora | Solomon | 78 |
| 32 | Kalbo | Retzina | Haim | 38 |
| 33 | " | Solomon | Haim | 5 |

| 34 | Kalbo | Bidu | Solomon | 82 |
|----|-------|------|---------|-----|
| 35 | Gabai | Isak | Mordu | 28 |
| 36 | " | Revekka | Isaak | 25 |
| 37 | Logia | Mois | Bohor | 52 |
| 38 | " | Sarra | Mois | 50 |
| 39 | " | Berta | Mois | 19 |
| 40 | " | Lazar | Mois | 14 |
| 41 | " | Siniori | Bohor | 78 |
| 42 | Litsi | Yakop | Bohor | 22 |
| 43 | " | Zibul | Yakop | 22 |
| 44 | " | Menahem | Yakop | 1 |
| 45 | Muskatel | Markos | Avraam | 62 |
| 46 | " | Buka | Markos | 62 |
| 47 | " | Leon | Markos | 35 |
| 48 | " | Viktoria | Leon | 33 |
| 49 | " | Markos | Leon | 9 |
| 50 | " | Tzenni | Leon | 7 |
| 51 | " | Albertos | Markos | 43 |
| 52 | " | Fortunè | Albertos | 40 |
| 53 | " | Markos | Albertos | 17 |
| 54 | " | Roza | Albertos | 13 |
| 55 | Menta | Bohor | Mordu | 65 |
| 56 | " | Mazalto | Bohor | 63 |
| 57 | " | Inta | Mordu | 57 |
| 58 | Muskatel | David | Markos | 38 |
| 59 | " | Ester | David | 34 |
| 60 | " | Rasel | David | 13 |
| 61 | " | Sarra | David | 11 |
| 62 | " | Zubul | David | 10 |
| 63 | Taranto | Bohor | Iakov | 59 |
| 64 | " | Sarra | Bohor | 63 |
| 65 | " | Klara | Bohor | 29 |
| 66 | " | Haim | Bohor | 28 |
| 67 | Tzivre | Elias | Siapat | 48 |
| 68 | " | Sarra | Elias | 38 |
| 69 | Mitrani | Solomon | Yoseph | 56 |
| 70 | " | Sultana | Solomon | 58 |
| 71 | " | Fortunè | Solomon | 23 |
| 72 | " | Aaron | Solomon | 21 |

| 73 | Dekalo | Mois | David | 38 |
|---|---|---|---|---|
| 74 | " | Retzina | Mois | 34 |
| 75 | " | Ester | Mois | 12 |
| 76 | " | Berta | Mois | 10 |
| 77 | Malki | Elias | Yoseph | 31 |
| 78 | " | Retzina | Elias | 33 |
| 79 | " | Yoseph | Elias | 11 |
| 80 | " | Mousis | Elias | 9 |
| 81 | " | Fortunè | Elias | 7 |
| 82 | " | Yoseph | Bohor | 60 |
| 83 | " | Fortunè | Yoseph | 47 |
| 84 | Muskatel | Solomon | Avraam | 50 |
| 85 | Taranto | Ester | Nissim | |
| 86 | " | Aaron | Nissim | |
| 87 | " | Sophia | Nissim | |
| 88 | " | Albertos | Nissim | |
| 89 | " | David | Nissim | |
| 90 | Messulam | Simanto/v/ | Isak | |
| 91 | " | Dina | Simanto | |
| 92 | " | Isak | Simanto | |
| 93 | " | Salvator | Simanto | |
| 94 | Ventura | Vitalis | Bohor | |
| 95 | " | Sarra | Vitalis | |
| 96 | " | Markos | Vitalis | |
| 97 | " | Retzina | Vitalis | |
| 98 | " | Samuel | Vitalis | |
| 99 | Tselebi | Alkabel | Mordu | |
| 100 | " | Inta | Tselebi | |
| 101 | " | Retzina | Tselebi | |
| 102 | Tzivre | Peppo | Haim | |
| 103 | " | Berta | Peppo | |
| 104 | " | Ester | Peppo | |
| 105 | " | Matilda | Peppo | |
| 106 | " | Nissim | Peppo | |
| 107 | " | Mois | Peppo | |
| 108 | Litsi | Marko | Solomon | |
| 109 | " | Zibil | Markos | |
| 110 | Alkabes | Yoseph | Samuel | |
| 111 | " | Reuna | Yoseph | |

| 112 | Alkabes | Isak | Yoseph | |
|---|---|---|---|---|
| 113 | " | Donna | Yoseph | |
| 114 | " | Matilta | Yoseph | |
| 115 | " | Prezenta | Yoseph | |
| 116 | Dekalo | Virtzini | Samuel | |
| 117 | " | Iakov | Samuel | |
| 118 | " | Nissim | Samuel | |
| 119 | Selik | Mordu | Mois | |
| 120 | " | Sarra | Mordu | |
| 121 | " | Revekka | Mordu | |
| 122 | " | Salvator | Mordu | |
| 123 | " | Klara | Mordu | |
| 124 | " | Zibul | Mordu | |
| 125 | Kazes | Albert | Isak | |
| 126 | " | Ester | Albertos | |
| 127 | " | Isak | Albertos | |
| 128 | " | Raphael | Albertos | |
| 129 | Tzivre | Peppo | Raphael | |
| 130 | " | Estir | Peppo | |
| 131 | " | Raphael | Peppo | |
| 132 | Kanetti | Avraam | Nissim | |
| 133 | " | Sophoula | Avram | |
| 133* | " | Nissim | Avram | |
| 134 | " | Liza | Avram | |
| 135 | " | Yoseph | Avram | |
| 136 | " | Mordu | Avraam | |
| 137 | Nahmias | Elias | Eliezer | |
| 138 | " | Luna | Elias | |
| 139 | Kazes | Aaron | Natan | |
| 140 | " | Renna | Aaron | |
| 141 | " | Natan | Aaron | |
| 142 | " | Solomon | Aaron | |
| 143 | " | Iakov | Aaron | |
| 144 | Mitrani | Yoseph | Solomon | 31 |
| 145 | " | Luna | Solomon | 23 |
| 146 | " | Sultana | Solomon | 1 |
| 147 | " | Sultana | Haim | |
| 148 | " | Ester | Haim | |

*The number 133 was assigned twice.

| 149 | Mitrani | Yuda | Haim | |
|-----|---------|------|------|---|
| 150 | " | Zibil | Haim | |
| 151 | Tzivres | Isaak | Siapat | |
| 152 | " | Neama | Isak | |
| 153 | " | Hazmonai | Isak | |
| 154 | " | Solomon | Isak | |
| 155 | " | Revekka | Isak | |
| 156 | Kassuto | Isak | Isoua | |
| 157 | " | Ines | Isak | |
| 158 | " | Berta | Isak | |
| 159 | Ventura | Samuel | David | 65 |
| 160 | Halphon | Israel | Nisim | |
| 161 | " | Revekka | Israel | |
| 162 | " | Samuel | Israel | |
| 163 | " | Dora | Israel | |
| 164 | " | Siapat | Nissim | |
| 165 | " | Ester | Siapat | |
| 166 | " | Dora | Siapat | |
| 167 | " | Soüla | Siapat | |
| 168 | Tzivre | Simanto | David | |
| 169 | " | Doretta | Simanto | |
| 170 | " | Ester | Simanto | |
| 171 | " | Roz-Mari | Simanto | |

# Selected Bibliography

A careful reading of the vast literature dealing with the camp experience will give the reader insight into the variety of Greek experiences during the period of German enslavement. Nearly every memoir includes at least one Greek story; such a phenomenon begs further study.

Attal, Robert. *Les Juifs de Grèce de l'expulsion d'Espagne à nos jours. Bibliographie.* Jerusalem, 1984.

Bowman, Steven. "Jews in Wartime Greece: A Select Annotated Bibliography." In *Greece in the 1940s: A Bibliographic Companion,* edited by John O. Iatrides. Hanover and London, 1981.

———. "Jews in Wartime Greece." *Jewish Social Studies* 48 (Winter 1986):45–62.

Chary, Frederick B. *The Bulgarian Jews and the Final Solution, 1940–1944.* Pittsburgh, 1972.

Czech, Danuta. "Deportation und Vernichtung der griechischen Juden im K. L. Auschwitz." *Hefte von Auschwitz* 2 (1970):5–37.

Franko, Hizkia. *Les Martyrs Juifs de Rhodes et Cos.* Elizabethville, Congo, 1952. Includes list of nearly all known victims.

Gilbert, Martin. *The Holocaust: A History of the Jews of Europe during the Second World War.* New York, 1985.

Hilberg, Raul. *The Destruction of European Jews.* Chicago, 1961. Constantly revised and augmented, this volume has become the standard reference for the German organization and implementation of the Final Solution.

*In Memoriam.* Hommage aux victimes juives des nazis en Grèce. Publié sous la direction de Michael Molho. 2nd édition revue et augmentée par Joseph Nehama. Thessalonica, 1973.

Kraus, Ota, and Erich Kulka. *The Death Factory: Document on Auschwitz.* London, 1966.

Lanzmann, Claude. *Shoah: An Oral History of the Holocaust.* New York, 1985.

Menasche, Albert. *Birkenau/Auschwitz II/. How 72,000 Greek Jews Perished.* New York, 1947. This is the first relation of the Greek tragedy in English and unfortunately is ignored by Holocaust researchers.

Müller, Filip. *Eyewitness Auschwitz: Three Years in the Gas Chambers.* New York, 1979. (Paperback repr., New York, 1984).

Novitch, Miriam. "End of Macedonia and Thrace Communities." *Ozar Yehudei Sepharad* [*Tesoro de los Judios Sefardies*], 4 (1961):liv–lvi.

———. *Le passage des barbares.* Jerusalem, 1982.

Sevillias, Errikos. *Athens-Auschwitz.* Translated by Nikos Stavroulakis. Athens, 1983.